Dress & Cloak Cutter:
WOMEN'S COSTUME 1877 – 1882

by Charles Hecklinger

Revised and Enlarged Edition

with additional material by R. L. Shep

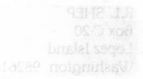

R. L. Shep
Lopez Island

ISBN 0-914046-06-3
LC# 87-042831

Printed in the United States of America

Published by:

R. L. SHEP
Box 668
Mendocino, CA 95460

Library of Congress Cataloging-in-Publication Data

Hecklinger, Charles.
    Dress and cloak cutter.

    1. Dressmaking--Pattern design. 2. Tailoring (Women's)
3. Costume--History--19th century. I. Title.
TT520.H455 1987   646'.47   87-42831
ISBN 0-914046-06-3

CONTENTS

Notes 1

Original Title 3

Preface 5

Introduction 7

Development of the Theory 9

The Measures 12

The Practical Drafting of Body Waists 20

Large Size Draft (Body-waist) 26

Body-waist Lengthened Below Waist-line 28

The Princess Style Dress 30

The Skirt 32

Short Sack Jacket 35

Loose Sacks 38

Loose Over-sack 39

The Long Over-sack 41

Walking Jacket 44

The Circular 47

Talmas, or Wraps 49

The Sleeved Talma 51

The Surtout 54

The Sleeve 57

The Dolman 61

The Gilded Age 69

Women's Costume: 1877-1882 71

The Etiquette of Dress 97

Glossary 114

Bibliography 120

NOTES

Charles Hecklinger's work was copyrighted in 1880 and published in 1881 by Root & Tinker, who were also the publishers of *The American Tailor & Cutter*. Claudia Kidwell, in her *Cutting a Fashionable Fit*, shows an edition of this work, also in 1881, which was privately printed in Burlington, Vermont. Hecklinger went on to write other tailoring books for women's clothes later in the 80's, and wrote at least one other book with J. O. Madison on cutting pantaloons.

Claudia Kidwell says that the first drafting system for women's clothing was a patent issued to Aaron A. Tentler of Philadelphia in 1841. Since women's clothes became quite tailored in the 1870's, the number of books written on this subject suddenly began to expand as tailors were able to develop systems by which to produce women's garments. Using Claudia Kidwell's chronology in *Cutting a Fashionable Fit*, we find very few women's tailoring books listed before the 1870's, and what amounts to a profusion of them by the 90's.

Hecklinger was a tailor and was writing for the trade, not for the home dressmaker, nor indeed for posterity. What were obvious fashions to him may well not be to us. His book is very straightforward and gives very simple cutting diagrams for basic garments. Even his own line drawings will show you that the fashions of the day were not that simple at all. He says this is a scientific system to give good construction as produced by a correct measure. The system actually is a combination of proportion and measure to give a proportionate draft by measure.

Drafts are given for the bodice (waist), or upper part of the dress, as well as the skirt; these stand on their own. Then he shows how to obtain a draft for a princess style dress by combining the two parts as princess style dresses were cut in panels from top to bottom without any cross-seam at the waistline. This is followed by drafts for a large number of outer garments: jackets, sacks, over-sacks, the circular, the Talma, the surtout, and the dolman. The outer garments are particularly interesting as they were not often shown in dressmaking books of the day. They also were worn for a much longer period both before and after the time we are attempting to cover, with few if any alterations being necessary.

The work is reproduced just as he wrote it with the exception of a few corrections where illustrations were obviously mis-numbered or reference to illustrations was left out of the text.

We have followed this with a very brief look at the times in the United States to help put the clothes into historical perspective. This is not an attempt to write a history book. There are a number of books listed in the bibliography which will provide interesting reading about this era for anyone who cares for a wider knowledge of it.

Similarly, in the following chapter on the clothes of the period, we have attempted only to discuss and show illustrations of some of the American fashions that were worn and not to go into minute details about their construction. Here again, enough reference is given in the bibliography to lead to further research for those who require it.

These chapters are followed by a long reprint from American etiquette books of the times which specifically refer to the Etiquette of Dress. This, then, is a reprint of a primary source and so should provide the best information on what was considered proper to wear on certain occasions. This material is also of interest to anyone who is doing research on the status of women in those times as it points up both their restrictions and many of their privileges, at least within certain social classes.

There follows an extensive 'Glossary', which seemed to be more necessary in this case than an index. Personally, I find it more than frustrating to attempt to do research in the costume field and find so few books with an index, and almost none with an adequate glossary. It becomes almost a case of "I know what this is, so you're supposed to know what this is, too". This is even more aggravating when the book you are looking at is over a hundred years old.

ACKNOWLEDGMENTS

I would like to acknowledge the vast amounts of help given to me on this project by the following people:

Pieter Bach, author and editor;
Helen Barglebaugh, editor of "The Costume Doll Quarterly";
Robert Kaufmann, librarian of The Costume Institute at the Metropolitan Museum of Art.

THE
DRESS AND CLOAK CUTTER.

A TREATISE ON THE

THEORY AND PRACTICE

OF CUTTING

DRESSES AND OVERGARMENTS

FOR LADIES.

ESPECIALLY DESIGNED AND ADAPTED

FOR TAILORS' AND DRESS-MAKERS' USE.

BY

CHARLES HECKLINGER.

PUBLISHED BY

ROOT & TINKER, 102 NASSAU STREET, NEW YORK.

1881.

PREFACE.

It is believed that the manner herein adopted of treating the Theory and Practice of the cutting of dresses is in a great measure new.

But few works of any value have been published on dress-cutting, and most of those consist merely of a few practical rules, without reference to any theoretical basis, and the author is not aware that the attempt to base the whole practice of the modern art on a sure fundamental principle, namely, the combination of a good construction as produced by a correct measure, has ever been attained.

It has often been urged that the cutter must apply the measure in connection with his draft; but this has usually been only given as an incidental maxim of practice; it has never been treated as the main principle of work from which success springs.

The nearest approach to this attempt, the author has met with, is in a little French work. This author makes the true principle consist in this, what he propounds as the novel method of combining the hight of the individual with his size around. But as he was unable, only in an approximate way, to perfect a collection of hights as a necessary means of carrying this combination principle into practice, he was obliged to form but an imperfect system, and therefore his work does not conform to true scientific knowledge.

The varied experience of the author leads him to believe that an exposition of the fundamental theory of construction will not only be satisfactory to accomplished cutters, by making clearer to them the principle he already acts upon, but will be found of still greater advantage in teaching those of limited experience.

The young student is often repelled from acquiring a scientific system, by thinking it complicated and difficult. Nothing can be more erroneous than such an idea: if learnt on proper principles it soon ceases to be difficult, and becomes an attractive study, and to attain moderate proficiency in it, is much easier than is usually supposed. But there are many cutters of more experience who are still much in the dark as to the true merits of the scientific principles and system, and it is desirable to impress on this large class how greatly the benefits to them would be increased if they would, by a little study, learn to cut and design in a more rational and systematic manner.

In the ever increasing competition in all branches of industry, the designing of Ladies' dress, also, has risen higher in the last years, to a standpoint more in conformity with the rules of art.

Unfortunately, the mass of dress-makers have not kept up with this progress, and many have not acquired these progressive principles. Many of them yet pursue the old taught system of superficial measuring, and teach cutting after the few uncertain patterns of ancient date.

Yet, sometimes they boast, with ostentation, to teach cutting thoroughly in a few days by a few rules, as if the structure of the body could be judged only by a measure of length or width? Endowed with superficial ideas and some paper cut patterns in their possession, they dismiss their scholars, even those who require practical skill to earn their bread as dress-makers.

To place before the dress-makers a change in this slovenly manner of work, the author undertakes to transfer the same principles in use among skilled artistic tailors, and to adapt it to the use of designing a garment for women.

Himself a practical tailor of a large and varied practice, he has endeavored, with the co-operation of many friends in the same line, to bring the art of dress-cutting to the standard of an exact science, and to make this science a common benefit to the whole mass of dress-makers.

Having been for years active in the literature of the clothing branch, he hopes to succeed fully in becoming intelligible in the necessary way of representation. The practical rules and directions given in the work, are all deduced strictly from our formed theory, are identical with those sanctioned by the best modern authorities, and adopted by the best modern cutters.

THE AUTHOR.

INTRODUCTION.

Dress-making is, without question, one of an artistic profession, and while it demands technical skill in putting together, it besides involves so much artistic taste as to call for the greatest mental energies and highest judgment of those engaged in it.

The artistic character of dresses call into action the best powers of the mind, in its intelligent study and practice. To investigate thoroughly its fundamental principles, we must bring to bear upon it, as we shall by and by have occasion to explain, reasoning of a high order. The observation must be keen, a considerable power of drawing inferences, and of tracing appearances to their causes, must be brought into use; and we must exercise judgment and taste, ingenuity of contrivance, and such a general course of thought and action as must, if it is to be successful, be dictated by competent and well trained mental powers.

The style changes continually; we may make hundreds of dresses, and yet no two similar ones may be called for. Each new one will possess some novel feature, offering special interest of the most diversified kind; sometimes it is the novelty of the goods, or the style, the demands of the customer, etc., give unbounded scope for artistic manipulation. Considering the great increasing demand for fine dress making, it is really astonishing to find how few take the pains to do it well. It has been remarked in our hearing, by one of the largest manufacturers, that good cutters are seldom to be met with—fine ones scarcely. And yet how amply it repays a little trouble devoted to its acquirement.

How then is this deficiency to be accounted for? Simply because it has never been admitted that dress cutting, like other branches of artistic knowledge, requires study. It is commonly supposed that after acquiring the simple construction of a waist, practice alone will suffice to make a good cutter. This is a great mistake, as experience abundantly shows. We continually meet with cutters who have practiced the greater part of their lives, and yet who, though they may be steadily occupied, work by such a crude system, to that sanctioned by experts in the art, as scarcely to be fit to be mentioned beside them.

We have already alluded to the wonderful variety of cutting and mode of construction. It is with this latter element that we have now more especially to do.

Although the construction of the draft is so simple that it might be learned in a few minutes, yet such is the scope that it gives for individual skill, that even with the same method it can be worked in a number of different ways, according to what the cutters notion of good cutting might be.

Now it is a natural inquiry, whether among so various modes and notions, differing so much from each other, there is not one in particular which may be identified and defined as superior to all others, and which consequently ought to be preferred for study? If so, what is it? What is the Theory on which it is based? And on what grounds does its superiority rest?

It is the object of the present work to endeavor to answer these questions: In the first place, is there any particular mode of constructing, which is so distinct and so superior to all others as to merit being distinguished as the best system?

This will commonly be denied, particularly by indifferent cutters, who will argue that opinions vary, that they think their own system as good as any, and so on. If they consider Dress Cutting merely a thing of chance, and one way as good as another, we have nothing to say to them, except that a good set of patterns would be better adapted to their capacity. But there are others more worthy of attention, who object to rules and system whatever, declaring that the draft ought to be by some such method as a chart which produces an even and regular pattern, and the cutters judgment alone, and their objection to systems is usually backed by the assertion that cutting by system is often unsuccessful.

The fact is, like almost everything else that may be done in different ways, there is a best way of cutting, and although a wide latitude may always be left for individual judgment and skill, yet the existence of a system of work preferable to all others, is sufficiently proved by its acknowledgement by all the best cutters, in a tolerably near agreement among them all, as to what this system is.

This system, as we have already said, essentially requires to be learnt and studied. It has been the result of long experience, and careful and intricate deduction, and it is scarcely possible for any one individual to arrive at the knowledge of it by his own practice or his own judgment, however shrewd, and he must be taught it, as students in other scientific branches are.

As no attempt has ever been made to work out and to explain the fundamental theory of construction, and believing that the thorough understanding of this is the best possible preparation for using the system aright, and for acquiring an intelligent style of cutting, we propose to state the theory fully, and show how it becomes developed in the shape of practical construction.

DEVELOPMENT OF THE THEORY.

In order that we may acquire the following illustrated problems, with the best hope of success, let us consider it as simplified by certain arbitrary limitations.

It may, in the first place, be asserted that by previous observation and experience, we may and commonly do arrive at some conclusion which enables us, with more or less confidence, to select from among the evidence some proof for holding to a certain opinion.

For example, we know that the proportionate size of a figure measuring say 34 breast, is invariably found in most points of relative ratio. This has been proved both by measuring the form and the deductions from the difference of build, with as much completeness as anything can be proved by these means.

If it is admitted that the figure is governed by a law of proportion, the invariable sequence of a certain size, then it is equally true that most all the sizes will correspond with its basis of measurement; namely, the "Breast Measure".

Granting the principle of the uniformity, what probability is there that in most cases the same proportion may exist?

It is evident, unless this probability exist in a high degree, amounting almost to practical certainty, that either the confidence with which we regard this law of proportion is greatly exagerated, or some one consideration which may exist in the uniformity of the figure has been omitted.

In all cases of induction, we can do no more than prove a certain law to be probable.

If our observation and experience be numerous and successful, the probability proved may be a high one, if few they may be slight.

Now it can hardly be doubted that we are correct in saying that by experience and subsequent induction we can arrive at nothing better than probability, and it is hardly worth while to enter into any study about how important a part this probability may exert.

And it is still more open to question whether a legitimate application of simple proportion, will permit us to hold belief with anything like that certainty, as many attach to it, even granting all the premises which they are in the habit of claiming.

Let us, in order to see the difference, turn to the basis of the modern method, which lies in the relation existing between the proportions of the body and its measure.

• It is a fundamental feature of the construction of this method, that these two, the proportion and the measure, are intended to act, not singly and independently, but in combination. And it is the full recognition of the fact, carried into all the ramifications of the drafts and designs, which characterizes the modern system, and give it its superiority over all others.

This is as yet but imperfectly appreciated by cutters who ignore this relation of the proportion and the measures; who rely mainly on a combination of lines and curves intended to give a draft of good proportion. Others will go further, giving some degree of consideration to the measures in rectifying the draft, but still making the proportionate standard the chief object.

The "Modern Theory," however, goes much farther. It carries the combined interest of the two to the fullest extent. It forbids consideration of one apart from the other, but commands treatment of both in strict conjunction—*in fact, to construct a proportionate draft by the measure.* For this object we establish certain natural lines on the body, which we need in the construction, and by which we are informed of the position, and the measures are taken to produce the size, and thus we obtain certain points by which our judgment is directed to the best advantage.

This principle of the combination of a proportionate basis and the measures is self evident, and none can doubt the resulting advantage. There are, however, two objections sometimes brought against it, which deserve brief notice.

First, it is said that "correctly proportioned garments, perfect in shape, handsome in outline, intended to fit only perfect forms, are regarded on general principles to give more satisfaction, and appear superior on an ill shaped form, and that using actual measures may lead one to sacrifice to a great extent the proportionate appearance."

This objection is merely founded on misapprehension as to how the principle is applied, for a study of the resulting system will show that it is fully calculated to realize any advantage the proportionate basis may possess, while whatever changes may be required according to measure, are only those where the draft is indubitably bettered thereby.

Then, secondly, it is objected that even with the measure, we do not always produce a correct fit—one which cannot be improved by trying on. But this involves a confusion in reasoning, For if indifferent cutters, whatever method used, the result would be equal; but if good practical workers, the additional help will give the advantage to those using the new method.

The fact is, however, that the general adoption of the principle should by no means supersede the exercise of judgment in its application.

The individual qualifications of the cutter will discriminate in cases where it may be proper to adhere to the proportionate method or not. Such cases may be of constant occurrence, but they do not affect the general advantage of the modern theory, which is sufficiently established on a sound basis, as the result of long experience.

Accepting, therefore, this system as the preferable one, we are able to enunciate the fundamental theory of the modern system, which is :—

That the proportionate build and measures shall be used combined; and that, in order to carry out most effectually this principle of combination, we adopt the measures as the most correct means to get a proportionate construction

THE MEASURES.

By Practical and Scientific Principles.

We now proceed to explain the measures—how to take them, and why such as are taken are practicable.

The measuring by the modern basis has for its object not only to obtain the length, or to locate the main points of the draft, but the measure aught to, at the same time, give us a comprehensive idea of the build and position of the figure.

By the relation of the back and front lengths as taken, we are at once informed if the figure is proportionate, erect or stooping, and this in connection with the blade measure, and the width of back, demonstrates to a certainty, and with no cavil of doubt, what the figure requires.

But as we take the measures we shall explain their value and relation to the draft.

The most important part, which we proceed to find is to locate two points from which to measure from and to. First, we find where the socket bone is at neck, and make a mark there with chalk. Then take the common square and lay it across the waist in such position that the long arm rest across the back, and the short arm over hips at side. Thus it must rest close down over the hip and held firmly and level at both back and hip.

While in this position we mark at back **0** and directly under arm at hip, as **F**, and at upper edge of the square at **C**, (see figure 1) : now these two marks give the level of bottom of waist at two important places, and it is necessary that care should be exercised in getting them correct.

1 THE BACK LENGTH.

Illustrated by Figure 1.

Now we come to measuring, which is first the back; for this we apply the tape at socket bone, and measure down to the mark at waist, which will give the actual length of the back. If the waist should be required longer than the natural waist and according to style, we also take the length wanted without removing the tape.

Next we apply the measure at the waist mark, and take the length to floor for skirt. In this case we pay no attention to the style, but merely get the actual length from waist to floor; for should a short dress be wanted we can deduct in the right proportion, and also add for trail.

Fig. 1.

2 FRONT LENGTH.

ILLUSTRATED ON FIGURE 2.

Is taken from the same point at back, down in front of shoulder to **F** at bottom of waist at side, level with mark, and from front of arm straight down. This measure is of great use, and must be taken correct, not too close on such shoulders as sink in at collar bone. It should not be drawn in too close at arm, but about 1 inch in front. Giving as it does the position, we cannot be too careful in taking it; it should be taken rather easy.

3 WIDTH OF BACK.

From centre seam of back **E** between shoulders to arm **P**. This must be the actual size without regard to shape of dress measured over.

4 ARM-HOLE SIZE.

Close round arm-hole, but easy.

5 HIGHT UNDER ARM.

The best way to take this is to have a small square made, which having a short measure attached at inside corner can be applied under arm, and close in front.

This square has also another tape fastened on its upper edge within two inches of front, and hanging down, by which to measure the length under arm.

Place this square under the arm so that it adhere close, but not so firm as to compel the person measured to raise the shoulder.

Hold it at back of arm with the left hand, and at the same time take hold of the tape with the right hand, and measure down to the mark at waist at **F**.

Also let the person extend her arm straight downwards, and measure to wrist for the length of sleeve, from **H** to **I**, (see figure 3.)

This measure of hight under arm gives a sure guide for showing if the arms, and therefore also the shoulders, are high up, or low down; as in the case of high shoulders, the measure will be longer than when low shoulders are the case, and in both cases the arm is located in different positions.

6 THE BLADE MEASURE.

ILLUSTRATED BY THE FIGURE 4.

While the square is in the same position, slip the tape backwards over the blade, taking notice that it is smooth, and measure to centre of back over the highest part of shoulder blade, and this must be taken close. This measure determines if the figure be full over blade or not, and in connection with front measure gives us a clear idea of the figure, whether erect or stooping.

Fig. 2.

7 BUST MEASURE.

The square being yet in the same position, by slipping the tape round to front, that it be straight and no wrinkles under arm, take the distance to centre of body, over the highest part of bosom, as shown on figure 5, from H to B. Let this last be taken loose.

8 BREAST MEASURE.

This is taken close under arm, around the body, over the fullest part of bosom and blade, and must be taken medium close—be sure in taking it that the tape does not drop below the shoulder blade, or it would give to small a measure, and with the view of preventing such an occurrence, it is better to stand behind the customer in taking it.

It being the measure by which some important points on the construction draft are produced, it will be evident that it needs careful attention. (see fig. 3.)

9 THE WAIST.

This we take around the smallest part of the waist, where it is defined the sharpest, and it should be taken rather close.

It is well to become proficient in taking all these measures in a correct way. Apply the tape smooth and even, neither close nor loose.

10 THE HIP MEASURE.

FIGURE 3.

Over the highest part of hip and closely taken, for all garments now worn are close to body.

Fig. 3.

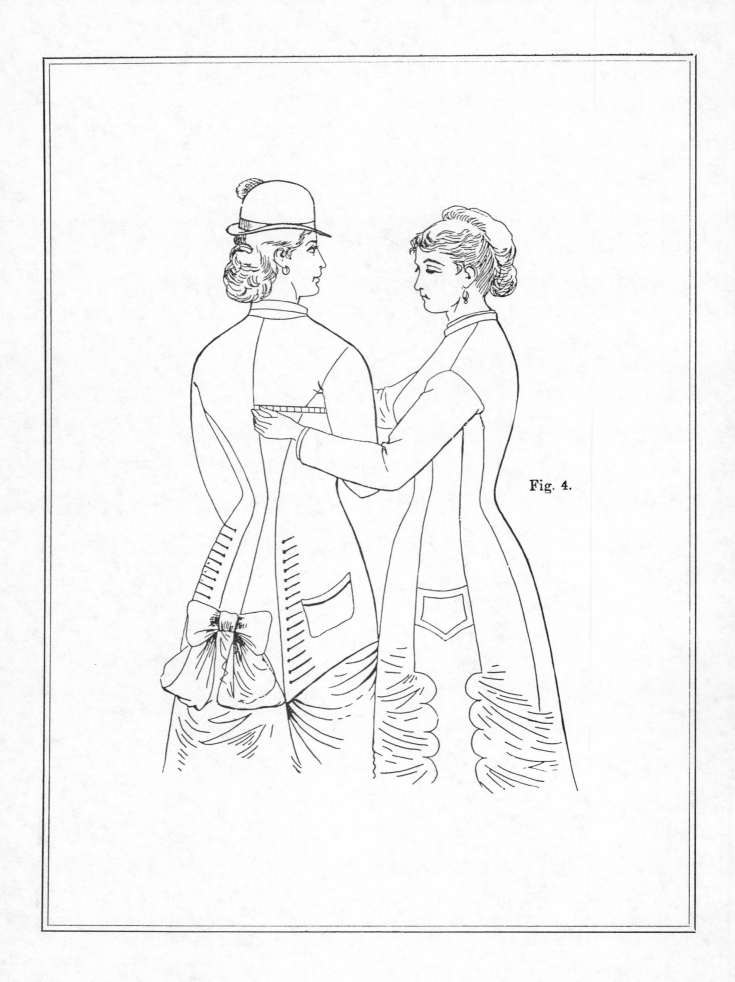

Fig. 4.

Fig. 5.

THE PRACTICAL DRAFTING OF BODY WAISTS,

By Measure as taken on the Body. Illustrated by Figs. 6, 7, 8, 9, 10.

We shall now begin to explain the system by which dress-waists are produced in conformity with the person measured: we shall try and make this clear by the use of diagrams illustrating every stage of drafting, and explain it so that none may go amiss.

In order that we may more intelligently proceed to work, we shall give a measure with which to draft this elementary pattern, and this measure being taken from a mass of such in our book, and one very nearly of good proportion, will be found as good an example to commence with as any.

The measure we shall use, is Breast 35, Waist 24, Back length $14\frac{1}{2}$, Width of back $6\frac{1}{4}$, Arm-hole 16, Length under arm 7, Front of arm or over blade $10\frac{1}{4}$. Front length $18\frac{1}{2}$. Now we first draw a line, about one inch from the edge of paper. It is always better, as it is easier to be drawn upon, to use pattern paper in order to produce the pattern, and far more economical than to draft it on the cloth, both in time and material.

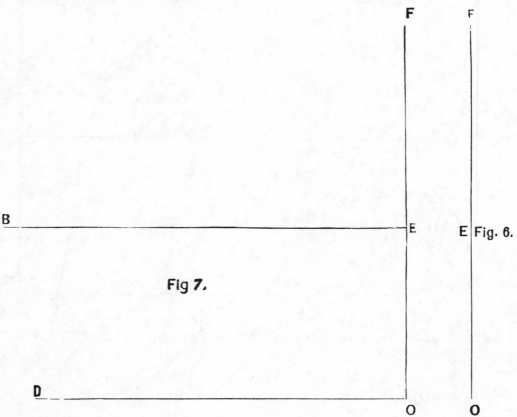

Fig 7.

Fig. 6.

Having drawn this line, as shown in figure 6, we make a point at its lower edge **O**, and at right angles with it draw another one to **D**. Next mark off from **O** upwards on front line, the distance measured for height under arm (5th meas ure) which is 7 inches, and dot **E**, (see figure 7). **From E** draw a line over to **B**, also at right angles with line **E C**. then measure from **E** over to **B** one-half of breast measure (35) equal **17½** inches; this one-half of breast measure is always sufficient for point **B** on all full grown forms and large persons, but when we draft for children or very indifferently developed forms, it is necessary to increase it ½ inch, this will make the draft easier for such form, and more nearly meeting the requirement of a slim build. Now place the tape at **B** and using point **E** as pivot, sweep down to **D**, where the sweep cut line **O D**, we make point **D**, (see fig-

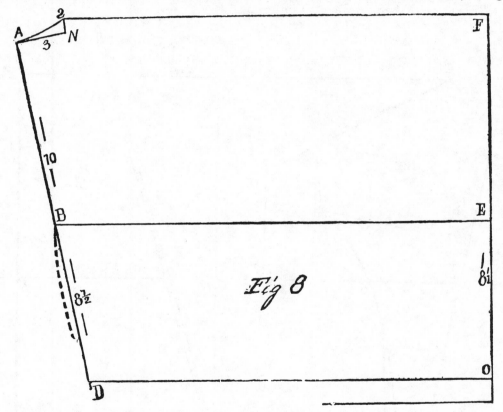

Fig 8

ure 8.) Next, place the straight edge on **D** and **B** and along it draw a line **D A**, which represents the centre of back. From **D** upwards measure the length of back (14¼ inches), and from **A** draw a line over to **N**, which latter is 2 inches over from **A**, then raise point 2 above **N** ½ inch and form the curve of back neck: now place the square on the front edge in such a manner that when the long arm reaches over it may just be at the same height as point 2, figure 8. This gives both front and back of one height, or as we might say in good proportion; but should the front be higher or lower, it would demonstrate a more erect or stooping position, according as the deviation may be more or less.

Let us now turn to figure 9, for a further illustration of the manner of drafting. From **B** to **H** on line under arm place the length of blade measure, or as mostly called by name of "front of arm"; this measure is $10\frac{1}{4}$. From **B** also forward is placed the width of back to **J**. In the centre between the points **J** and **H** mark **I** and draw perpendicular lines up at the three points. Then from **I** upwards to **R** place one-quarter of the arm-hole measure (16) which is 4 inches, and from **R** to 2 on top of back draw a straight line.

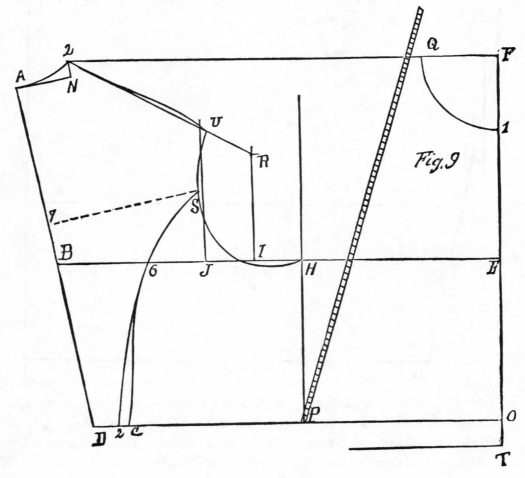

The next step we will take, is to draw the back; first by **curving** the shoulder line above straight line $\frac{1}{2}$ inch. near arm-hole, and **curving** back to line again near **2**, and also from **U** form arm-hole towards **S** where it runs over the straight line, thence curving downwards and below **I**, $\frac{1}{2}$ inch to **H**; we draw this line inside at **S** because by measuring from 7 we find the measure to reach less than to the line, generally $\frac{1}{4}$ inch. We make the back at bottom $1\frac{1}{2}$ to 2 inches wide, and draw the side seam from thence to **S**.

As style has greatly to do with the shape of the back, we can here give only an average shape as an example. The seam however is changeable to any position, without affecting the fit of the waist in the least.

From **6** at blade form sidebody to within $\frac{1}{2}$ inch of back **2**, which gives **C**; now place the front measure from **P** up towards **Q**, deducting from it the width of back, and make a short sweep at **Q**. From line at **F** measure over to sweep at **Q** one-eighth of breast measure for proportionate build, $2\frac{1}{4}$ inches, and $1\frac{1}{4}$ inch more.

In practice we can use the neck measure, which in most cases is easily arrived at without taking it, for the majority of such sizes measure 15 inches. Should the neck appear slim, 14 comes nearer; if short and stout, 16 would answer better. Yet for some garments it is essential to have the neck size in order to construct the waist close to measure. Of the neck we use $\frac{1}{2}$ of the diameter. From **F** square with front draw a line, either above or below as the measure happens to give it, to intersect sweep at point **Q**. Then sweep from corner **F** by **Q** to **1**, for neck. Measure from point **U** around the armhole past **S**, **1** and **H** to 16, the size of arm, and fix a point at 16. (See fig. 10.)

Take the width of **back** shoulder and place it from **Q** towards 16, and fix point, then curve front shoulder and finish, say by going out beyond 10 a suitable distance to make the arm-hole look a good shape, or about $\frac{3}{4}$ inch.

Form neck by dropping it $\frac{1}{2}$ to $\frac{3}{4}$ inch to **Y**. Then from **Y**, which is $\frac{1}{4}$ inch inside of front line, curve out towards **E** $\frac{1}{2}$ inch beyond the line, then going back over line, draw it inside $\frac{1}{4}$ inch to **T**. Measure from **Q** to **T** the front length, less width of back, and 1 inch below it draw a straight line as from **T** to 11. We can also take a measure down to bottom of waist at front, to get the correct length and apply it from **Q** to **T**.

In the middle from **E** and **H**, mark a point **5**—and also in the middle between 5 and **H** mark point **8**.

Now we have come to the most difficult **part of the dress**—waist designing which is placing the darts in their proper places.

We shall take a proportionate build, and place them **accordingly.** **Later** on we shall show under what conditions they require changing in position, yet the manner of getting their size is the same in all cases, suitable and in harmony with the measure.

We have a size of waist of 24 inches, one-half of which is 12. Now we find by measuring the line **O O**, that it is 15 inches, while it ought to be only 12, or one-half the waist measure. The size deducted from the length **O O**, gives the value to be taken out in one or more darts.

If, as in the case of many men, there were no taper to the waist, there would be no darts needed ; but as in every case of female form, the difference between the size of breast and waist is considerable, then it becomes evident that this difference must be removed by darts, in order that the waist may set close.

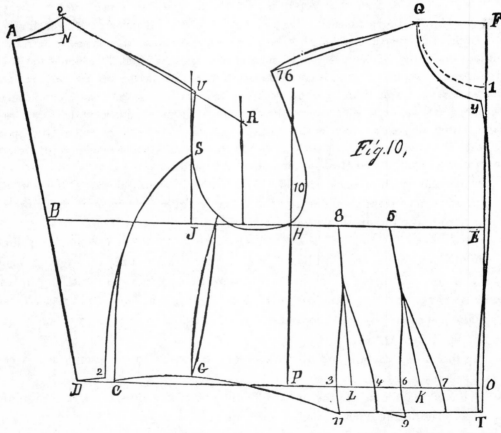

As this difference between these two sizes determines the value of the darts, it s evident that the fuller the bosom, and smaller the waist, the larger will be the darts; and in a contrary case, the flatter the breast, as compared to the waist, the smaller they are needed.

As we have already stated that the size of the waist should be 12 inches, which deducted from the length **D O** leaves 3 inches, these are taken out in 2 darts, each of a size of one-half of these 3 inches, or equal to $1\frac{1}{2}$ inch each. Now where shall we place them? Divide the space between **P O** into 3 parts, which gives points **K** and **L**. From **5** draw a line to **K**. From **8** one to **L**.

Then place the size of darts equally on each side of line, that is $\frac{3}{4}$ of an inch from **K** to **7** and **K** to **6**; also from **L** to **3** and **4**, and draw them like the diagram. They should not reach up over $\frac{2}{3}$ of the distance from **K** to **5**. The one nearest arm-hole can be $\frac{1}{2}$ inch higher.

Now it remains only to finish the waist line from **11** to **C**, running it $\frac{1}{4}$ above line at **G**. Also drop point **9** one-quarter below.

Then divide the side-body from about the centre between **J** and **I** to **G**, taking out $\frac{1}{2}$ inch curve.

This concludes drafting the waist to measure; and as every size, whatever the measure, is produced identically the same, only deviating in so far as the measures may be of different sizes and lengths.

As regards the darts, we may add a few words to what we have said about them while drafting. On a well-proportionate form, we never find such a wasp-like waist as some persons consider so desirable. On this measure we have a breast of 35 inches, and a waist of corresponding size of 24 inches, yet it often happens that persons of the same breast-measure possess a much slenderer waist, even down to 20 inches, which indicates a bosom uncommonly developed, and which makes the difference between the upper and lower width so strongly marked.

Then the darts become necessarily larger, and sometimes 3 are inserted.

On a full bosom the darts should be cut high; on flat, they are needed lower, and placed more back at top. Cut well forward below, produces the effect of small waist. Cut back they give a fuller shape.

LARGE SIZE DRAFT.

FIG. 11.

The manner of drafting this, as well as all kinds of waist-patterns, being similar to those already explained, it seems quite unnecessary to go over any lengthy discussion.

We will only make clearer some few points in regard to drafts of large sizes.

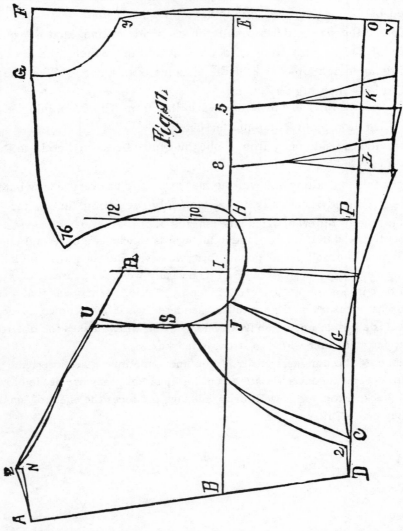

The points being produced by measures, by the same process as used in drafting figures 8 and 10. But one point we must be careful about, which is never to cut the shoulder broad on such large sizes. In fact, it never is necessary to go over and outside of the line at **U** above **S** for width of shoulder.

And again, as the measure by which this draft was reduced is: Breast 42½; waist 34; length of back 15; width of back 7¼; arm-hole 18; size over blade to front of arm 12⅓; height under arm 6, and front length 20, we get a size corresponding to the increased measure. We find also that the distance of line **D O** being 20, and half the waist but **17**, an excess of 3 inches to be taken out in darts at front.

Then again, the space between back and first dart being so great in large sizes, it will answer better to get a close, smooth fit, to put in two cuts, one at **G,** and one somewhat forward of **G** and between **G** and **P.** This will enable the waist to fit closer over and along the waist.

It is also well to take the length from top to bottom at front on these sizes, in order to better regulate the correct place it should be cut to.

In the matter of darts, in order that the form may appear to better advantage, it seems right to place the darts so that they reach well up. This will close up better on bosom—a form most necessary on this build.

When the size of bosom is excessive, as it will generally be found in such large sizes, than 3 darts are necessary.

On this form as well as all the waist patterns cut in this manner, we add the seams when cutting out the material, for the dress must be when made up exactly the correct breast measure and ½ inch more.

Body-waist Lengthened Below Waist-line.

Fig. 12.

This diagram shows two different shapes at the bottom. These deviations of shapes are easily produced, and need no particular explanation.

But to lengthen the waist so that it will be of a size to correspond with the size of the hips, and to put the amount in the right place, is what we shall now make clear.

Clinging to our idea of thorough completeness in our work, before giving the way of extra increase of size of hips, which on all proportionate forms is generally 12 inches over waist, we shall find where this extra increase is met with. We will take the standard of waist proportion to be 12 inches less than hips, so that a waist of 24 inches would be accompanied with hips measuring 36. This would not always hold good, and some would say that a greater difference would be the general formation, but in the strictest proportionate figure, our figures would be right. Supposing then this difference to be 12 inches, there would be 6 inches on a side to be added.

This amount is not distributed all around, neither is it distributed alike in each individual, still the forms are so similar in a large number of cases, that a rule may be laid down which will suit a large majority of forms.

The rule is that the largest amount of increase is at the sides, that one-half of the increase is at 7, 8, 9 and 10, and one-fourth each at front and back.

Now figure 12 shows a draft for designing one of an increase in length. We there have 3 inches to be added on one side, and $1\frac{1}{2}$ inches at back and $1\frac{1}{2}$ at front.

From **0** to **B** we go out to hip down $\frac{1}{2}$ inch on back of seam, and the same amount of curve on the side seams. On the side body seams which join the back, we add $\frac{1}{2}$ inch for a good curve.

At front the line is run along the straight line as on the diagram, with scarcely any increase to speak of; but the darts are drawn down each seam, having a curve of $1\frac{1}{2}$ inch.

Now it remains only to add on the side-body seam. This will be, as we have a sum of 3 inches to dispose of, giving a strong outward curve of $1\frac{1}{2}$ inch.

When a great amount of increase is needed, it is always desirable to cut the side-body narrow, and make another cut farther forward, like **I J**. In this case the amount of hip size can be divided between the two openings, giving $1\frac{1}{2}$ for each. The bottom can be regulated to fancy or style.

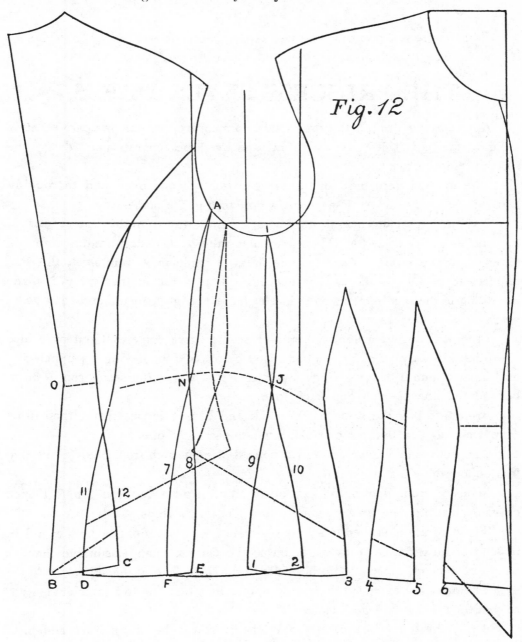

Fig. 12

THE PRINCESS STYLE DRESS.

After having drafted the dress-waist to measure, we cut it apart—that is separate the back side-body and front, and by those separate parts design the skirt for this garment.

The method here used ought to be carefully gone over and thoroughly learned, for every sack style garment is produced in the same way.

Lay the back pattern against a line at **O**, and away from this line at waist at **B**, 2 inches. (See fig. 15.) Then draw along the back pattern, and also from **B** to length at **C** a straight line. If the dress is made in a train skirt, this line requires to be lengthened as it is needed. The width at the bottom is made according to the requirements of a close or loose fitting garment, and may be an average of 12 inches.

From **E** to **D** draw a line, and on both seams curve somewhat out over hip.

The side-body (Fig. 14,) is laid also against a line, having its upper part on line at **A**, and **D** being $1\frac{1}{2}$ inch away from it. Curve the seam from **D** down beyond the line $1\frac{1}{4}$ inch and back to **B**.

From **B** to **C** is the same as the back and 2 or 3 inches more, then draw from waist to **C** a line curving also over the straight one.

The front is laid down as shown, point **C** being 1 inch from line. From **C** to **D** at bottom draw a straight line.

Measure from **D** over to **E**, 25 inches, and draw a line from **E** to **E**, thence curve over at hip near **H** very strongly for room for the hips.

The diagram is drafted to a shape very nearly proportionate, and would in its length and width be an average, but as the fashion changes suitable changes would be needed, especially in the width of the lower end of the skirt.

The darts are extended down below waist line, tapering to a sufficient length, so that they will give a good shape.

Apply the hip measure, and make the dress 2 inches more, then add on or take off on the side-seams, to accord with it.

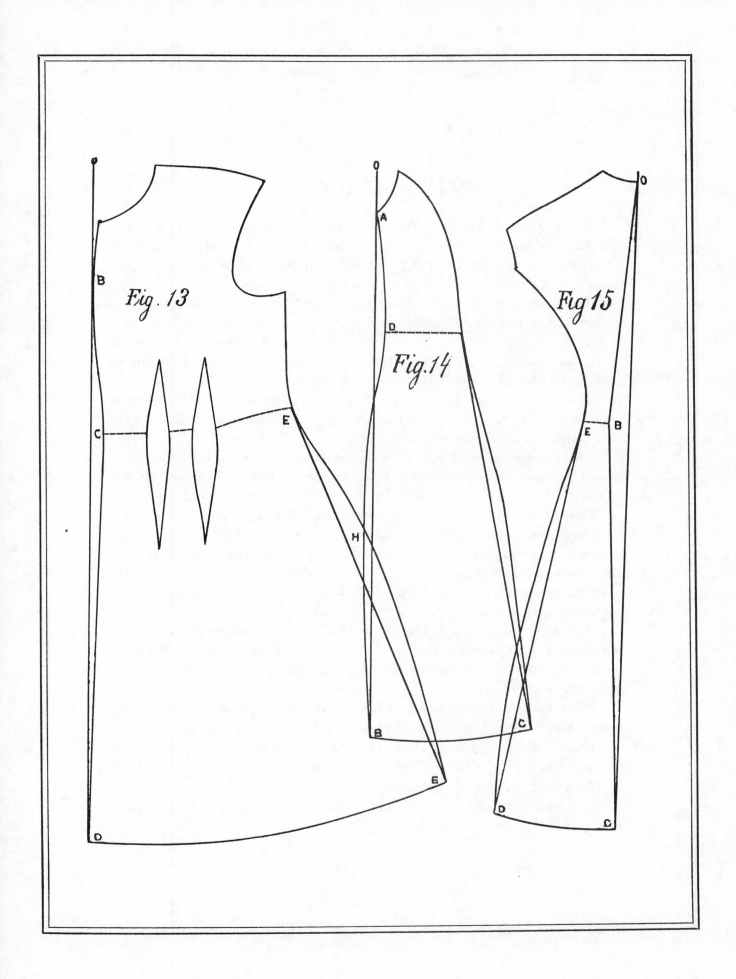

Fig. 13

Fig. 14

Fig 15

THE SKIRT.

The drafting of skirts for dresses is a subject which has not been so clearly and fully defined in text books. to my mind, as might be. Most all theorists have their own peculiar point of producing a pattern, some of which are quite wanting in a sound basis, either as regards balance or shape.

The much superior way of producing a skirt, in order to attain a perfect balance and correct shape, is, undoubtedly, a mode similar to that used by tailors in cutting the skirts of coats. Such a one, we have always found, would answer every call made upon it, and give a skirt superior in hang and shape, and always ready to be adapted to any style, however changeable.

The diagram Figs. 16 and 17 will give an illustration of the manner in which a skirt is drafted, and the following explanation will be sufficient for a clear understanding of the method:

First draw a line like **O B**. Then lay the pattern of front of waist on the line in such a position that the middle of breast be close to line, as at **A**, and the bottom at waist $\frac{1}{2}$ away from it at **D**, in fact in the same position as when drafted.

Now from shoulder point as pivot, sweep from **R** to front for top line. **R** is the lowest waist point on side. Then lay the square on the front line so that the short arm may run over and touch the curved line near **2**, second dart, then draw along it for upper edge.

Next measure the length of skirt from **E** at square line down to **B** for full length of skirt.

Although the measure is taken at the back, yet we find the variation to be so little that it will answer equally as well for the length in front. Yet some prefer, while measuring, to take the length in front as well, which, of course, gives additional security.

From **X** as pivot sweep **B** to **S** and **P**. The size at bottom is regulated by style. This for a medium size of 36 breast, would be $1\frac{1}{4}$ yard from **B** to **P**.

Some ladies even prefer a skirt so scant as only to measure $2\frac{1}{4}$ yards in the whole circumference, which indeed is rather small.

It is, of course, self evident that stout ladies would in the same ratio need a size of 3 yards or over, as the size of the person is large, or the desire is for a roomy garment.

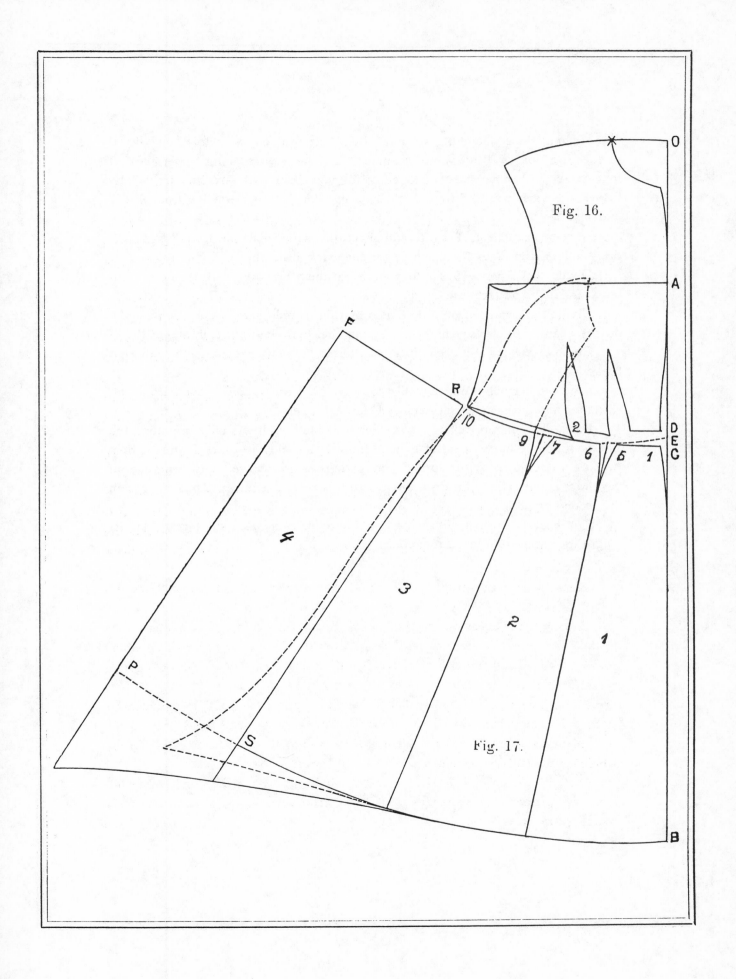

Fig. 16.

Fig. 17.

Having placed point **P**, we put a long straight edge on to **P** and lay it in the direction of **F**.   While so placed lay the square along upper part of long edge, and move the two together till you form a square line from **P** by **F** to **R** on waist point of front.   Then draw along its upper edge from **R** to **F** and also to **P**.

Now measure from **F** to **R**, and place the same distance from **P** to **S**, and draw a line from **S** to **R**, which is for the back breadth.

Divide the distance **S B** into 3 parts for the 3 breadths.   Break off at front top at **C** ½ inch and form the curve.

Divide the distance from **R** to **E** also in 3 parts and mark them.   Then take out the quantity of darts, whatever they may be, between **5, 6, 7, 9,** and at **10**.

Curve the seams and draw lines from top to bottom to separate the different breadths.

This manner will produce a skirt for a walking dress, and is the base for all skirts, or any garment which reaches below the knee.

For a skirt longer at back, or a train, this method differs only in putting the side-body on the upper seam of skirt in the manner shown by the diagram; then running a line down by the spring, and giving a slight curve, and springing out beyond **S** to the extent of train wanted.   In this case it requires to be longer from the second breadth back.

The back is drafted with a straight line, the same as a short skirt, but its length increased from line **S** to conform with it.

SHORT SACK JACKET.

Fig. 19.

In cutting sacks, the first consideration is a good balance, and in order to attain this, there is nor never can be a better guide than the body-pattern to follow. In using this, if it be good, we retain all its good points, and get the same certainty of fit as we would in case of a dress-waist.

We take, for instance, the pattern of the back, lay it on a straight line like fig. 18, so that the upper corner at the neck rests on the line at **0**, and the lower part be, for regular built, 1½ inch away from the line as shown at **C**.

Now trace all along the pattern, following closely the edges. Then from **0** at neck, measure down the length desired, and from 1 to 2 inches above **C** begin to curve gradually out toward the straight line—this should be a continuous curve.

The style of these jackets being close, and for giving a narrower effect, it is well not to make the back too wide; for this reason make the bottom from **B** to **E** 6 inches. From the point at waist 1, draw curved line to **E**.

If the garment is intended to be heavy and used as an over-garment, certain additions are required at top, on back, on shoulder and at sleeve, ¼ inch. From **F** commence adding with ¼ inch, increasing it till at **D** we add 1 inch. From **D** curve the line to **E**.

Draw a line, and place the side-body against it, with point **H** resting on it, and the waist being 1 inch from **B**. (See fig. 20.) In cases where the hips are very large, the the distance from **B** is 1½ inch.

Now trace the side-body, and from **D** at waist, measure the length as produced by the back, then curve the side-line from **D** to **A**.

Having got the right length, fix a point in the centre between **D** and 1 at waist, and from it as pivot sweep from **A** to **N**. From 1 to **N** draw a straight line, then curve over it considerably at hips, in order to have room for them.

Make the bottom of side-body as wide as the back.

When the back is cut 1 inch from **D** at waist, and it is intended as an outside garment, it is always well to take a little of the width of the side, therefore then go in at **D** on the side-body ½ inch, and then curve the side line.

The front (fig 21,) is drawn in the following way. Draw a straight line, like from **0** to **E**. Lay the front pattern against it, when intended for a thin garment, but for a heavy one, let it be ¾ of an inch from it at breast, and 1 inch at waist.

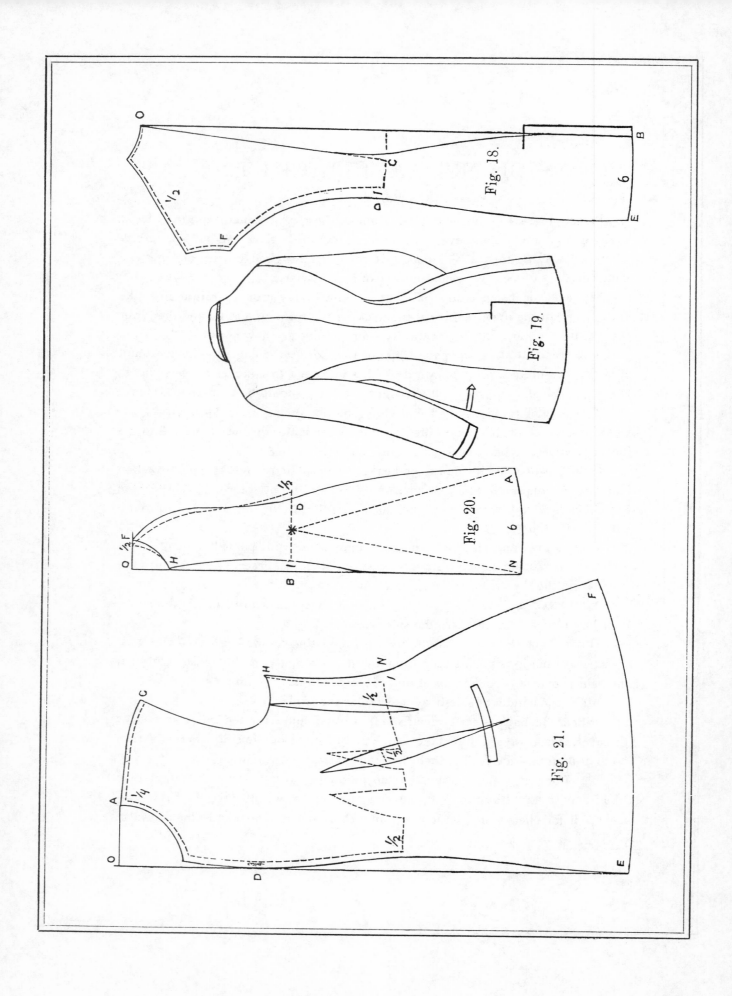

Fig. 18.

Fig. 19.

Fig. 20.

Fig. 21.

Now trace the edges of the pattern. From the waist in front draw a line to bottom at **E**. Place the side body from **H** to **N**, and by it get the length to **F** wherever it may be.

From shoulder point **A** as a pivot, sweep from **F** over to **E**. For an overgarment add on at shoulder ¼ inch, the same at neck, one-quarter at **H**, going out at **N** 1 inch.

Now take the measure of the hip; find out how much the back and sidebody measure as they are cut, then apply the balance from the front over towards the side. This measure gives the width the sack ought to be, and must be the full measure and 2 inches over for seams and ease. This will give a point below **N**. Then from **N** through this last point draw a line to the bottom at **F**.

Draw in the same darts, or when it is not wanted close one is used, and then it running more forward at top.

Sometimes also a cut is taken out under the arm of ½ inch size.

We have said to move the side-body out at top from ½ inch to **F**, this will be found correct on heavy goods only; but on light material, keep the form the same as the original pattern.

If a close short sack basque or jacket is desired, it is far better to start the dart in front, and draw straight down parallel with the front to the bottom. Thus the skirt will cling closer to the form, and produce a more elegant fit.

LOOSE SACKS.

Figs. 22 and 23.

In continuation of our endeavor of giving every style of cut, the diagrams **22** and **23**, illustrate the manner of drafting a loose sack, such a garment **as is** usually worn for a morning jacket, and well adapted also for an out-door garment, when made out of suitable material.

This, like all our designs, is drafted by the body pattern, which is laid on to a line at **0** and 2 inches away from this line at the waist. Next measure down and fix the point where the length is wanted, as at 6. Now from **0** draw along the back to 2, and next with a graceful curve to point 6.

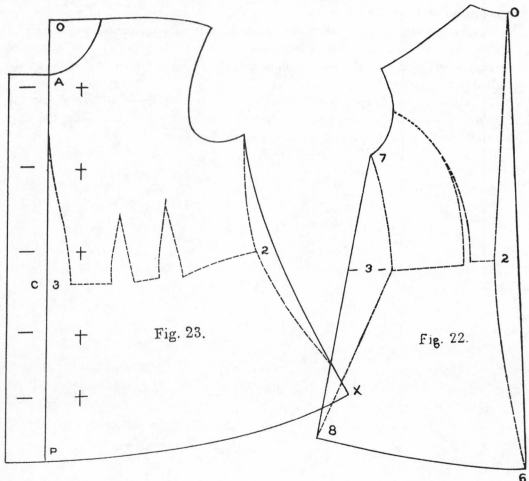

Fig. 23.   Fig. 22.

From **O** as a pivot sweep from 6 over to 8. Now lay the side body against the back in a similar position as it occupied when being drafted, and draw along the pattern on top of back, over the shoulder, along the arm to 7.

Make a point from the waist, 3 inches, as shown on the diagram, and then from 7 through 3 draw a line to 8. This gives the back for a loose sack.

Should we want one closer fitting, we adopt the same means, but only make it closer in size at the waist, and after drawing the line from 7 to 8, we also draw one from the lower waist point of the side-body to 8, and cut the pattern out by this last line, which gives one having a close fit at waist, and yet giving enough material to cover the hips and the skirt well.

In drafting the front, take the body-pattern and lay it on the line so that it may touch at **A** on top of the front at neck, and let the waist be 3 inches or $2\frac{1}{2}$ inches away from the line at **C**.

Now trace all along the pattern at neck—over shoulder—along the the arm hole.

For a loose sack we add 2 inches over the body-pattern at 2, lower waist point at side, while for a close sack we draw from 2 to **X**. It is evident point **X** is got by first placing 2 inches at waist, and then drawing the line for the loose garment.

Next apply the back along the front, which locates the length of the side-seam on the front. Then sweep the bottom from the shoulder point as a pivot.

Add the lap in front $1\frac{1}{2}$ inches for single, and $2\frac{1}{2}$ inches for double-breasted.

LOOSE OVER-SACK.

FIGS. 24 AND 25.

We here introduce a plate of a Loose Over-sack, which is cut long and suitable for a Water-proof.

The similarity of this with figs. 22 and 23 is so close that it seems hardly necessary to give any added description. Yet we will show where the difference lies. The back is laid away from the line 2 inches at waist, and 3 inches on the side. Over the back and shoulder, also on the arm, there is added, for an over garment of light material, $\frac{1}{4}$ of an inch, and for one of heavy $\frac{1}{2}$ of an inch. From **P**, where it is $\frac{1}{2}$ inch larger, we draw a straight line through 3 inches to bottom.

At front we lay the pattern $\frac{1}{2}$ inch from line at breast, and 4 inches at waist.

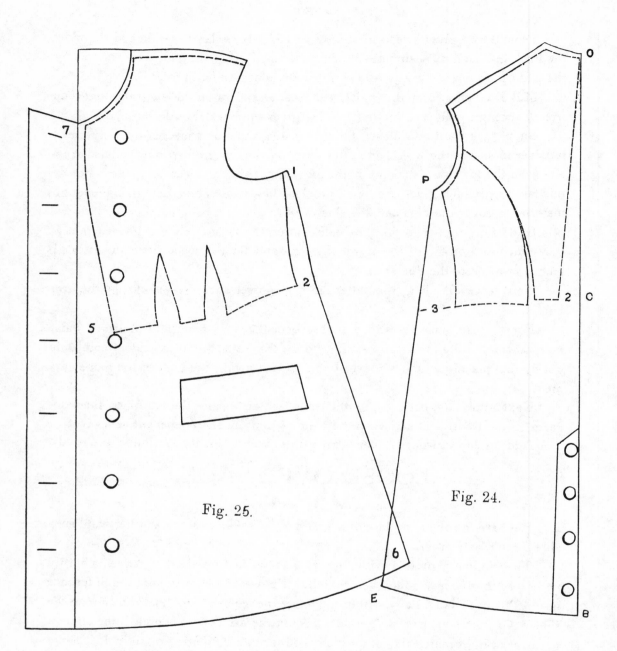

Fig. 25.

Fig. 24.

Then add on shoulder ½ inch. One inch at 1 on side, and 2 at waist; then draw the line, curving it out below 2, to give a little more cloth to 6. Sweep for bottom for shoulder point. Add on in front for double-breasted beyond the line 3½ inches; for single-breasted 2 inches. Put in a plait at back with buttons. **Have** buttons close together, and let them run down to the bottom in front.

THE LONG OVER-SACK.

Cut by the Body-Pattern. Figs. 26, 27, 28, and 29.

In cutting a long sack, two points have to be decided: First, what must be added for extra size; and second, how much skirt is needed over hips to set well. Garments made of light, thin material require less size than those of thick heavy goods, and therefore the cutter's judgment is used to decide what additions should be made.

But let us begin to draft. Draw a line like **O B.** Then lay the pattern of back, resting on a line at **O** and 1½ inches from line at **C.** (See fig. 26.) Now trace the back seam, and slightly curve it below **C** down to **B.** From **O** apply length wanted down to bottom, at **B.** From **O** sweep over from **B** to **F,** and make **F** 6 inches from **B.**

The size I give is for narrow skirt, such as are worn now, but can be increased if a broad back is desired.

At **R** add 1 inch over back pattern, which makes back wider and better suitable for this style of garment. At **O E D** add ¼ inch for thin goods, ½ for heavy. Then shape the back as per diagram. At line **O** over the hips both seams are curved a trifle over the straight line.

The addition in width at **E** and **D** on back is calculated for an ordinary proportionate person; but on flat-backed, very erect built, never add any extra width between the shoulders, for an over-garment, for if it is done, it will surely be pushed back by the arm. This is because it requires no more width to cover a flat surface; but on a round back, on the contrary, we must add more because that will take up more.

The Side-Body. Fig. 27.

On a straight line place the side-body, touching at **S,** and one inch from line at bottom **E.** Then draw from **S** along side-body to **I** and **F,** curving over hips. Should the hips be full, make the distance from **E** one and a half inches to **I.**

The side-body point **D** is moved over ¼ inch, and from **D** we draw the blade line coming in ½ inch at bottom **H.** Make bottom **F** to **A** 6 inches.

Apply the back at **D** and find the length; then at centre **H E** sweep for bottom.

The Front. Fig. 28.

On a straight line lay the pattern so that the centre of front rests within ½ inch of line, and bottom **K** 1 inch, then trace along sye **E** to **C,** and from **C** draw the side seam 1 inch outside of **N.**

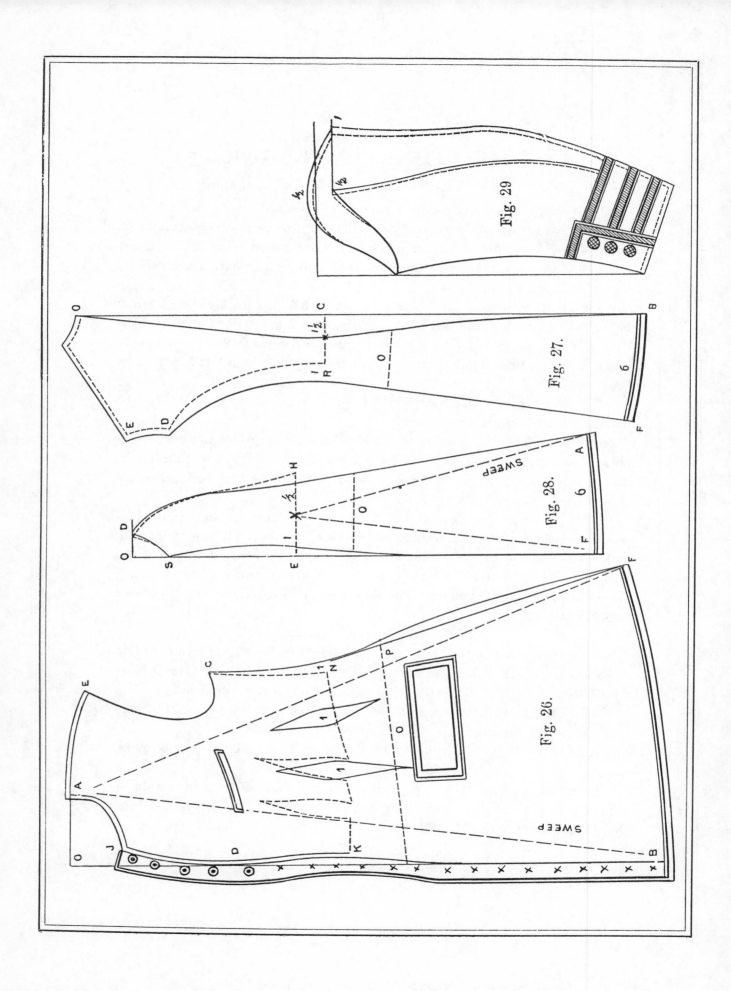

Fig. 29

Fig. 27.

Fig. 28.

Fig. 26.

Next lay the side-body on **C**, and **N** on **F** to get length.   Then measure over hips on the back and side-body as cut, and lay the balance of the measure on front, adding on 2 inches extra, and get point **P**; now from **N** through **P**, draw a line, and curve beyond it $\frac{1}{2}$ inch for the side-seam.

Add on shoulder $\frac{1}{2}$ inch, advance point **A** $\frac{1}{4}$ inch and form gorge to **J**. Sweep from **A** as pivot by **F** for bottom to **B**.

Draw front line **J D K** to **B** $\frac{1}{2}$ over front, and then add for lapel for single or double-breasted, according to the style wanted.

Place darts farther back, (see fig. 3,) and make them $\frac{1}{2}$ inch less in size.

THE SLEEVE.   FIG. 29.

The addition on this is 1 inch on back seam, $\frac{1}{2}$ on top and $\frac{1}{2}$ inch on lower sleeve seam. also $\frac{1}{2}$ longer, as shown on diagram.

WALKING JACKET.

FIGS. 30 to 34.

The smart looking jacket of which is given a design as it looks when done, is now much worn, especially by young ladies. It therefore should have a smart appearance, which can be produced by finely shaped lines. With this in view it becomes necessary that the seams in the back should have no sudden round over side-body, but only a gradual curve.

The seam on shoulder must be high up. To produce a good close-fitting skirt, it is necessary that the lower edge or bottom, cling in to the dress, for when it sticks out it detracts from the style and spoils the whole garment.

In order to produce a skirt with these essential qualifications, the top line from **R** to back plait is dropped down 1 inch from sweep. The waist seam is made 1 inch longer, and this extra is shrunk in, giving more room over the hips, and preventing the tendency of gaping behind.

Our diagram gives a double-breasted jacket; this, as is evident, can be changed to a single or to any style of cut-away.

In order to produce the pattern, having all the good qualities of a fit, we take the body-pattern, as cut to any measure. Of this pattern we place the back on a line previously drawn on paper, touching at **O**, and moving **C** at bottom of the waist away from the line 1½ inch. Then curve the back seam a little above **C**, adding over **C** ¼ inch, thence running down to **B** at bottom to length wanted.

In measuring for jackets, always take, besides the natural waist length, also an extra length where it would appear best that the seam should be; this is the most prominent part of the hips, and is generally 4 to 5 inches below the waist.

This extra length of waist seam is placed from the waist pattern down from **C** to the hook.

As this is an over garment, we allow ⅛ to ½ of an inch for making up, as the goods may be of light or heavy material. From **O** on top of back, on shoulder and at arm hole add this amount over waist-pattern. At **F** add a trifle, going down to **D**, which latter point is 1 inch from the pattern, thence with a slight curve to the bottom at **E**. The distance from **B** to **E** is about 5 inches.

Then add also for the plait and hook. Before proceeding further, let us observe that on a flat back the width of back must not be increased at **F**.

Next take the side-body, which place against a straight line, point **H** touching at this line, and the waist point being 1 inch from line at **B**, for all ordinary

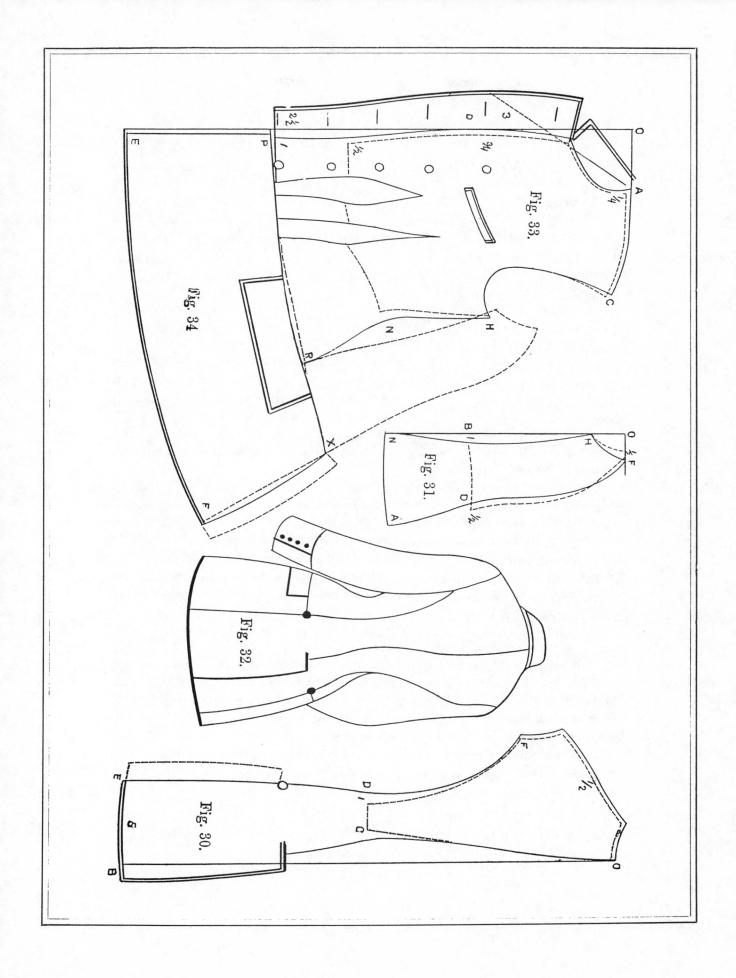

Fig. 33.

Fig. 34

Fig. 31.

Fig. 32.

Fig. 30.

forms. But on all such forms whose increase of hips is more than 10 inches over the waist, we move the waist away from the line at this point $1\frac{1}{2}$ inch. Then draw along the side body from H to 1 and N, touching line at N. The distance down from B to N is regulated by the length on back from D to button.

The top of the side-body point is moved over to F $\frac{1}{4}$ to $\frac{1}{2}$ inch, then from F draw the seam touching at the full round of the blade, and from thence gradually go inside until we arrive at a point $\frac{1}{2}$ inch inside of lower point of side body at D, and down with a slight outward curve to A. Now apply the length of back and rectify that of the side-body.

THE FOREPART. FIGS. 33 AND 34.

Draw a line O E, and on it lay the front, so that it is within $\frac{1}{2}$ inch of the line at breast, and 1 inch at waist. Then draw the front line outside of the body-pattern, $\frac{1}{2}$ inch; this will give extra width to the jacket, all along from top to bottom. Draw also the neck along the seam; then the shoulder, adding $\frac{1}{4}$ inch to C; thence along the arm-hole to H. At H we add $\frac{1}{2}$ inch, and at N a seam.

Draw the darts, extending them downward, by curving below like our diag., giving not too much curve, and leaving the piece between the darts pretty nearly straight. From N to R spring out the line.

Next take the hip measure, and deducting from it the width of the back and side-body, apply it at 1 in front, and measure to R, adding to the measure 2 inches, and moving point R in or out to the size.

Now apply the side-body at H down to R, to get the correct length, and leave it in a closing position touching at R and up along the seam an inch or two. Then from A, top of shoulder point as pivot, sweep from middle of side-body, past R to the front. Lay the square at front line, and touching at first dart, draw the sweep straight from thence forward.

Then add for lapel, making it $2\frac{1}{2}$ inches at waist, 3 inches at breast at top. Also further regulate the front shoulder by the back.

Also raise the skirt seam $\frac{1}{2}$ higher near R, so that it will be a continuous curve.

From R to back plait we change the sweep by curving it downward 1 inch below the sweep at X. Then place the side-body on this changed line in a closing position on waist seam, and draw the plait line by laying the square on the spring of the side-body and along it draw the plait to the bottom F.

Now measure the length by the back, and sweep the bottom from F to the front by A, also curve $\frac{1}{4}$ over line.

THE CIRCULAR.

Fig. 35.

This garment, although made up in a variety of different styles and shapes, still in all will retain the simple construction, as given in the diagram.

In order to design them, the waist pattern is also used as base to work from. This is laid on a straight line close at **D** and about two inches inside of line at bottom of back, **C**.

Then place the front closing at sleeve head on shoulder **E**, and placed so that a right-angled line from **O** will run along the front to **K**.

For a very large, loose garment, having a great deal of drapery hanging down from the shoulder, we can move the front pattern out more, still letting it touch at **E** closely to back, which of course causes point **P** to come closer to back. Then we will have to draw the front line from **S** front of breast to **K**, leaving always about 1 inch distance from **J**.

For a close-hanging garment, the opposite to this is done, and the pattern is moved the other way; that is, closer towards the centre, which causes point **P** to be farther away from back. The front line then is drawn by the front, and the balance drafted by the same manner one as another. Now trace along the pattern for the top of back, and both shoulders and neck, to **R**.

Then draw a line from back point to **P**, on front shoulder point and dot between the two points in the centre. From this centre make a line to **E**.

Next measure the length desired from **D** on back to **B**, or wherever it may reach to. Then sweep the lower edge from **B** to front at **K** by **F** as pivot. This circle needs straightening both at back and at front, square with front and back line, as shown at **B** and **K**.

From **R** to **S** we retain the curve of front pattern, thence the front is taken along the straight line to bottom.

Whatever size, and whether close or loose-cut circular is drafted, the point **L** is always the pivot for the lower circular edge.

Sometimes it is advisable to cut them with a seam running over shoulder down through the centre to bottom. Then the centre of the back is laid on the fold of the goods, which obviates a seam in back.

These slight modifications can easily be determined without further explanation, and to any practical cutter any variations may at once occur.

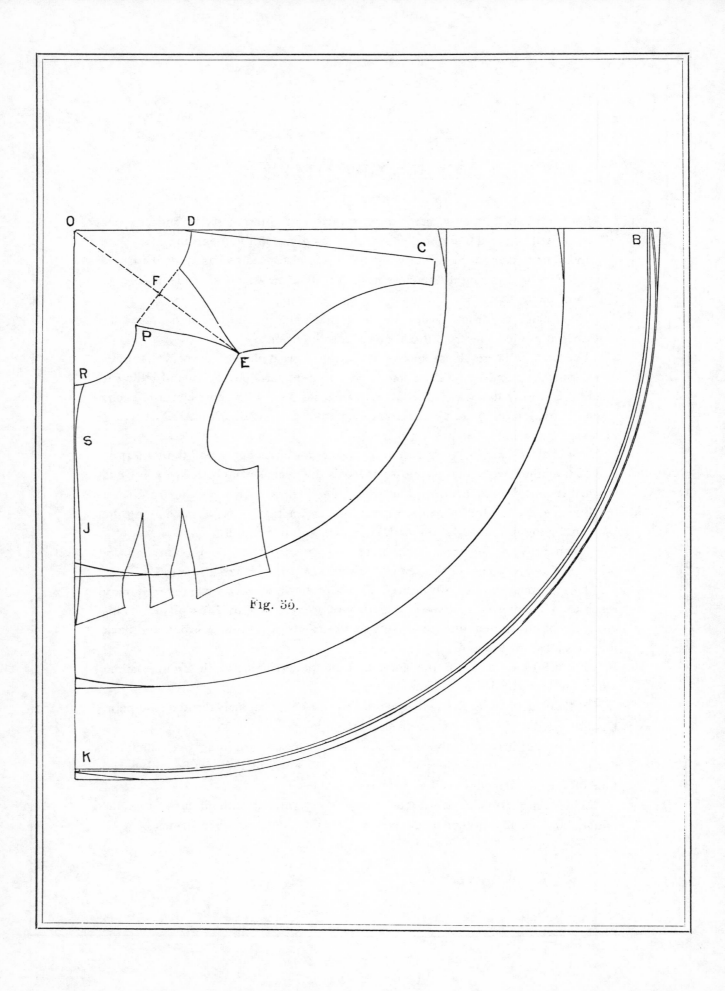

Fig. 30.

TALMAS, OR WRAPS,

FIG. 36,

Are, in general construction, similar to a circular, as regards the shoulders and neck, and also the covering for the back. Therefore a method identical is used in designing them.

The only difference is attributable to the front, where it is cut either with taps coming down low and cut square, or when it is cut the same in shape at front as at the back.

After the pattern has been laid on the line, we follow along it to the waist, and then curve it to line again.

Draft the shoulders and neck, and when it is intended to come to the front, we simply follow that of the waist pattern, and form the lower part in any shape we desire, while the back may retain the shape we have designed on the diagram.

However, when we want one cut in a very close form, and simply hanging down from the shoulder, then the front line deviates so far, that it starts from the shoulder point, and takes the curve of front to waist, thence curving inwards to bottom, similar in shape to our diagram.

It is difficult to give any close rule to adhere to in forming this garment. The only point is the shoulders, which must be produced by the shoulders of the body-pattern; the lower points are as yet only a matter of taste, and must be produced by the judgment, and there are such a variety of different changes, that it would be impossible, in a work of such limits as this, to give more than a general idea.

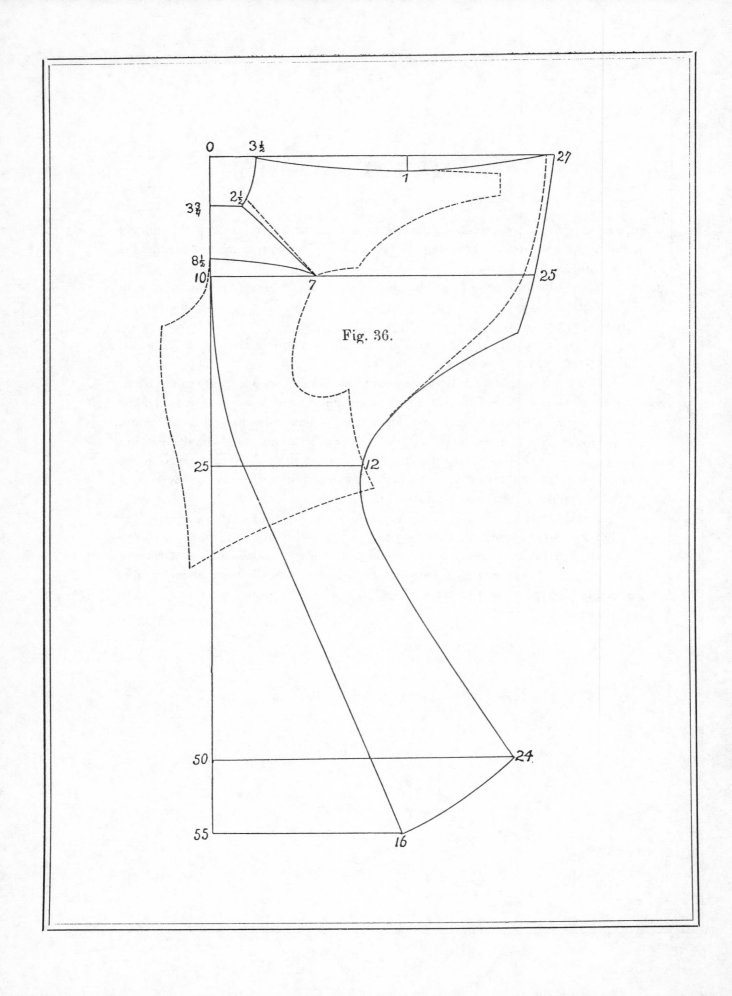

Fig. 36.

THE SLEEVED TALMA.

FIGS. 37 AND 38.

The garment here represented takes on more the nature of the Dolman ; but as it is one made generally of light summer goods, and merely a wrap, it may be placed in the same class as Talmas proper. It has, as will be seen, the French back and a circular, loose sleeve.

In order to draft it, we use the body pattern, and we may again state that no manner of drafting gives such a guaranty of fit and ease in working as this.

Lay the back on a straight line touching at 0, and 1 inch from D. Then draw along the pattern from 1 to 1. Apply the length wanted to C. From 1 to C draw a straight line.

Also draw along top of back and shoulder. Then make the back at D as wide as the style should make it, say 3 inches. Then at C to F place 5 inches. Now from B draw a nice curved line to E and F.

Next place your sleeve pattern in such position, notch of sleeve on the back notch, and when a wide sleeve is wanted swing the lower part of the sleeve farther out from back, and when a close sleeve is desired, nearer to back. An ordinary distance is when it is in such a position that from S to back at one it may measure 24 inches. Having placed the sleeve as wanted, draw from B along the top of the sleeve, making it a little scanter than sleeve-head at front, and curving down along front seem to S.

Now from shoulder point of back in front of 0 as pivot, sweep from S ; or if it is wanted that the sleeve should come down to the bottom of the back, then sweep from F, when it will probably come to S 0. Then draft the shape of bottom as may be desired, but be sure not to make the front any longer than pattern sleeve at S. This will produce the sleeve and the back in one piece. Should it be desired to have the French back, then draw from B towards E, and at E take out a space of 1 inch, thence to nothing at F.

It should always be borne in mind, whatever the style, be sure and not retain the full round of sleeve head, but, on the contrary, take off the round in front, only retaining the height, which is essential, otherwise it would pull down on the shoulder.

Turning now to the front, lay the front pattern of waist model against a line previously drawn on the paper, and let it touch on the middle of the breast, as at 0, and be $1\frac{1}{2}$ inch away from line at waist H.

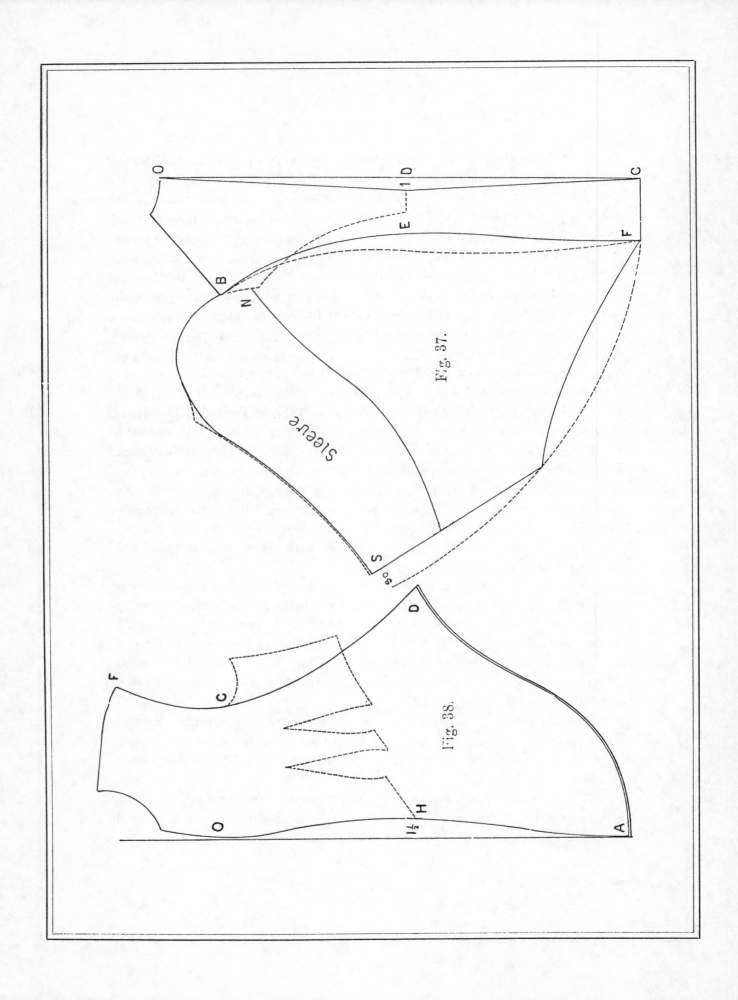

Fig. 37.

Sleeve

Fig. 38.

Now trace along the pattern, retaining the same front, neck, shoulder and arm-hole seams. Now lay the sleeve on the back, (we mean the loose sleeve just drafted,) so that the exact point where the front arm seam comes, which ought to be notched, will rest on **C**. This is found by measuring the sleeve head. We allow for fullness of top **1** inch. Now supposing this sleeve head measured 8 inches, we would measure off from **F** on front shoulder to **C**, **7** inches; leaving the **1** inch to be worked in on top of the sleeve. Make a dot on **C**, place the sleeve on **C**, notch on dot, and swing the bottom out to **D**. This will be easily determined if nearly far enough, for a curved line drawn along the side seam of forepart, from under the arm to waist, and thence sprung out, as is customary for hips, will bring it about right.

Then mark the length by the length of sleeve, for where the lower part at **S** comes to is found point **D**.

Now curve your bottom line of front to suit any shape desired. The front is made in many different ways—it may be cut perfectly circular; or longer at **A**; or again straight across from **D** towards the front, about half-way, and then making a square-shape piece of point **A**.

THE SURTOUT.

PLATE 39.

THE BACK. FIG. 1.

Take the waist pattern and lay it on a straight edge at **0**, and 1½ inch in from line at bottom of back. (See fig. 1.) Draw the back line along back to 1½, thence down to **D**. Now measure from **0** to **D**, the extended waist, and to **E** full length. Draw from **D** to **E** a straight line, leaving 1 inch for tack at **D**.

Next add over pattern at top ¼ inch, on shoulder ½ inch, at scye ¼ for flat back, for round ½ inch.

At bottom we make the back wider by adding 1½ inch at **A**, and from **A** to **F** draw a straight line, then curve it at **R** ½ inch over straight line.

From **E** to **F** make the back skirt 5 inches.

THE SIDE-BODY. FIG. 2.

Draw a straight line and lay **C** of the side-body on it at top, and 1 inch away from it at waist. Then draw the outlines. Then from **C** draw the side seam along side-body, but ½ inch outside from it at 1, thence curving to **F**.

From **P** run along the side-body, and curve it ½ inch inside at natural waist, and curving out for spring to **E**. Finish the line at bottom from **E** to **F**.

THE FRONT. FIG. 3.

First draw a straight line like **0** and **B**. Then lay the pattern so that the upper part of breast lay within ½ inch of it, and 1 inch away at **S**. Now draw the front line of breast from top ½ from and larger than waist pattern, to **S** and **D**.

Also draw the shoulder, making it ½ over pattern, and also add ¼ at shoulder point, and ½ along at neck near lapel. Draw the scye; at **N** add ½ inch, to 1 inch for ease at waist 1; thence curving out to **E**.

Make the darts the same size, adding only seams.

Now lay side seam of side-body on to front to get the length at **E**. Having the length, sweep from **E** to **D** at front, making shoulder-point the pivot, then let the front be square with front line from first dart to **D**.

Extend the darts down to bottom of front, giving each seam a slight curve, as shown in the diagram to give it shape. Now last apply the hip measure to see if the size is correct; should the draft be too small add on at **E** more round, and on side body at **F** also.

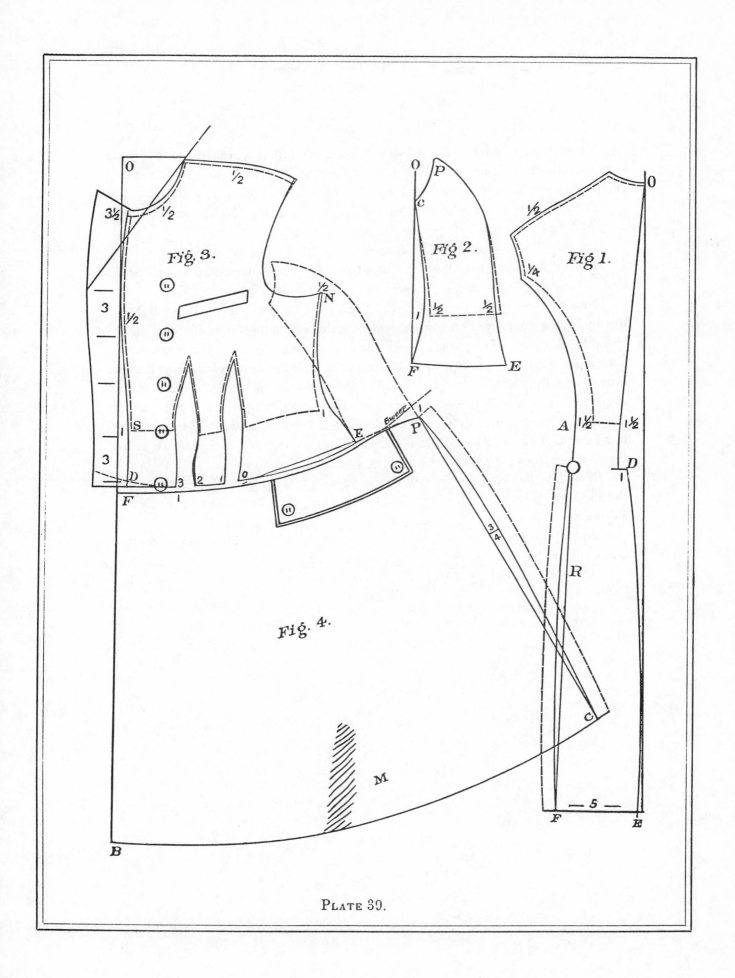

Fig. 3.

Fig 2.

Fig 1.

Fig. 4.

Plate 39.

Never spring point **E** on side-body much, as ladies' garments do not bear it at that point. Some ladies are full in front, especially those who are stout built; such would need more round added on the darts at **0** and **1**, **2** and **3**.

For single-breasted add over front line 1½ to 2 inches. Double-breasted add on 3 at breast, 2½ at waist 3 inches at lapel for lap.

The Skirt. Fig. 4.

Extend the front line down to **F** and **B**, Lay the front pattern as produced by the foregoing, in such a position as shown in the diagram.

Now first sweep from point **E** to **F**. This sweep will run above **F**; straighten this by laying the square on front line at **F** and touching sweep at first dart.

As the skirts by this style are made just scant enough to cover the dress, without surplus fullness, we must curve the upper seam more downwards from **E** to **P**, instead of following the sweep. By following and making the upper seam of the shape of sweep, our skirt would be apt, when done, to hang in a fold at bottom at **M**, which it ought never to do. Therefore point **P** is lowered below the sweep ¾ to **1** inch as shown. Also add on above the sweep a curve of ½ inch between points **E** and **0** just above the flap, which gives a better shape.

Now lay the side-body on this line, and with the straight edge placed along the spring of side-body, draw the line from **P** to **C,** then curve out over this line for the plait, ¾ of inch.

Apply the length of back to get the length of skirt. Then sweep for the bottom from the shoulder point, which finishes the surtout.

The sleeve is enlarged like all for over-garments.

THE SLEEVE.

Figs. 40 and 41.

Every one knows that the sleeve facilitates or hinders the movement of the arm : but many are not aware that it may be the cause of a general derangement of the " *waist*," when badly cut or put in the arm-hole.

To produce all the good qualities required in a perfect sleeve, carefulness must be used while cutting it, that it be based on the form of the arm-hole, and in harmony with the position of the form.

The " conditions of a perfect sleeve " are, 1st, that it must be just the length of the measure taken, to the wrist, where the wearer prefers it, a thing impossible by any other way of measuring than ours; 2d, when the arm hangs natural, it must touch in front at the cuff at wrist, and any extra width produced by fashion must be added, and should hang back; 3d, the top of the sleeve requires to be of a size proportionate to that of the arm-hole, to enable the wearer to raise her arm horrizontal without too great a strain upwards on the waist, and thus causing a drag; 4th, when the arm is at rest, the top should curve around like a cylinder, and not lay flat—this can be produced by a judicious distribution of the fullness.

The curved line that forms the top of the sleeve is not the result of a capricious inspiration, but an operation based on geometrical principles. For an explicit and comprehensive demonstration of the theory on which sleeves are designed, and the particular shape inherent to them, would require more space than is at our disposal and belongs to a more elaborate work ; yet our explanations will give a sufficient guide for all practical purposes.

The Manner of Drafting Sleeves.

We can see by looking on the diagram, fig. 40, that the sleeve is bounded in front and back by the perpendicular lines, which on all proportionate shapes are apart one-half of the scye. And that from the line under the arm, which is the breast-line, to the line at top, **R**, is one-fourth.

This square we adopt as a guide in drafting the sleeve. We first draw line **0** 16, and square at top line **0 B**. Now from **0** we go down one-fourth of arm-hole, which is for a 16 scye 4 inches to point 4.

Now divide this distance into 4 parts, which will make them apart 1 inch, and draw lines across at every point. Next, from **O** to **B** is ½ of scye, or in this case 8 inches. Now draw a line from 4 to **B**, and make point **C** in the middle from the two points. From thence draw a short straight line to **H**, square with line 4 **B**. **H** is from **C** one-third of the scye, or 2¾ inches.

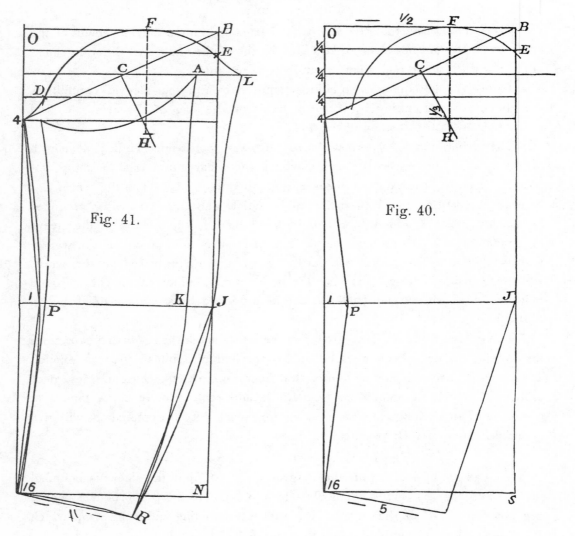

Fig. 41.

Fig. 40.

Now take the tape, and **H** as pivot, sweep the top curve from **F** each way. **F** is just above **H** in a perpendicular line.

Now from 4 measure length of arm (16) to point 16. At half the distance make line 1–J, and dot in at 1 one inch to form the front lines by. Also draw back lines from B down to N parallel with front. Square with line P 16 draw line for bottom and make width to style (5 inches.)

Now turn to diagram 41 ; finish top curve from D to 4 and E to L which must be on line A L, in a slight curve. Curve the front and back seams like diagram.

From D straight down draw a line to P for lower sleeve, and curve it so that it will be ½ inch inside of top sleeve at P coming to 16.

The distance gone out from E to L is placed inside from E to A to get point A. Now draw undersleeve from A to front near 4, dropping ¼ below line.

Draw from A down a line perpendicular to K, thence to R.

The sleeve must be close as that is the prevailing style, and should be curved in some below L and A.

Point E sews in on back notch, and point 4 at front, they being half of the sleeve, with some added for fullness at top. To retain the back seam at E down, start from E and below it curve in, coming back to J thence to R. Start the lower sleeve at 4 and curve up towards A, then measure under sleeve from 4 to A just ½ of scye and ½ inch for seams, and then run line down from A parallel with upper seam to K, thence gradually wearing towards R.

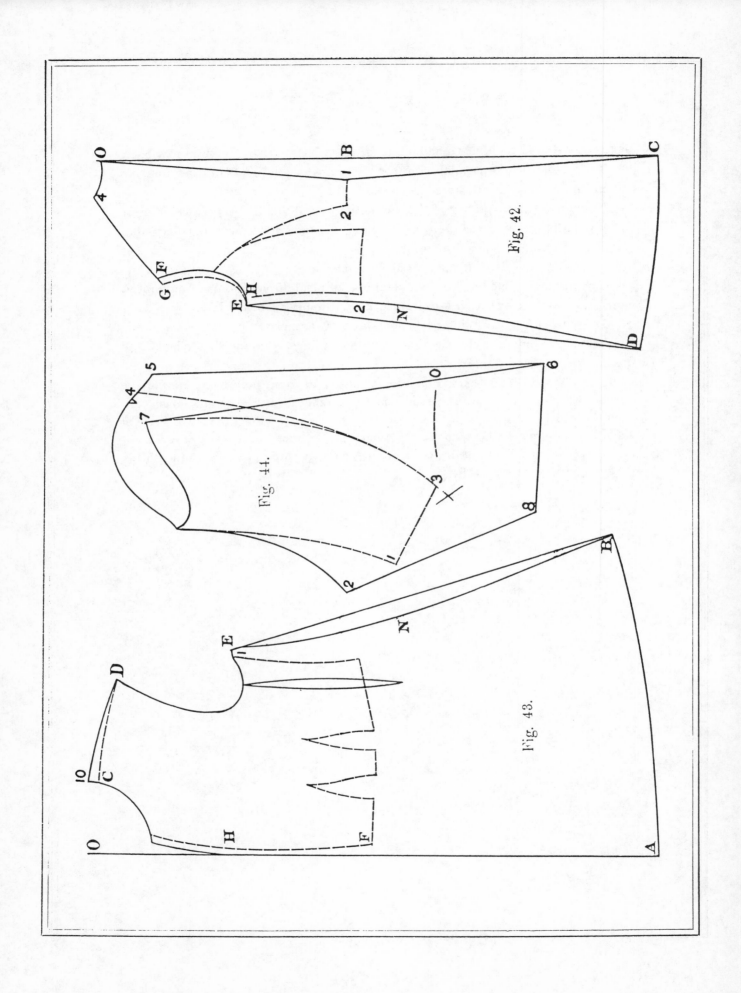

Fig. 42.

Fig. 44.

Fig. 43.

THE DOLMAN.

Of all the garments which are usually made by tailors, the one presenting the greatest difficulties, both to the cutter and the maker, is undoubtedly the " Dolman." That is to say, when it should fit well and be well made.

The difficulties are associated with special features, which may almost be said to belong entirely to this garment. To begin with, the dolman is a loose wrap, and yet it should give the form of the body. On many a piece of tape is placed inside at back, in order to tie around the waist, and hold it close to the body, yet it must have such a form in the back, as will retain the peculiar cut, more striking in this than any other garment.

The shoulder, in order to place the sleeve seam in the proper place, high up, must be cut narrow, which counteracts the tendency of the sloping form of shoulder, so liable to occur more on this than any other outside garment.

The sleeve should have just the right proportion of fullness, so that it may hang gracefully without drawing. The front should also be narrow, so that the swing of sleeve be forward, and although the leading features must take on more or less the same form in each garment, yet there is, perhaps, none with greater variety of style in the various details as round and square sleeve.

In order to overcome the several difficulties in designing this, let us, first of all, take up the original " Dolman," which is a loose sack form, with a flowing sleeve. By commencing with this, we will acquire the principle more readily, and thus be better able to design intelligently any other style.

As will be seen on diag. 42, the back is laid on a line at **0**, and 1 inch from it at **B**. From **0** to **C** place the back length as wanted. Now lay the side-body against the back, close at top, and about 1 inch from it at waist, point **2**.

From 1 opposite **B** to **C** draw a straight line, and trace along the back pattern from **0** to 4 and **F**, **F** is ½ inch inside of pattern at point **G**, making the shoulder narrower. Draw from **F** around arm-hole to **H**. From **H** side-body point of pattern to **E** is ½ inch. From lower side point at 2 place outwards 1 inch and dot.

Now from **E** through dot at 2 draw a straight line, which will reach to **D**. From 4 as pivot, sweep lower line from **C** to **D** curve along ½ inch from side-body part **N** to **D**.

We now take the forepart, diag. 43, and lay it within ½ inch of line at **H**, centre of breast, and 1½ inch away from it at **F**. While in this position trace along the edges of the pattern, so that it will be marked out on the paper. Then

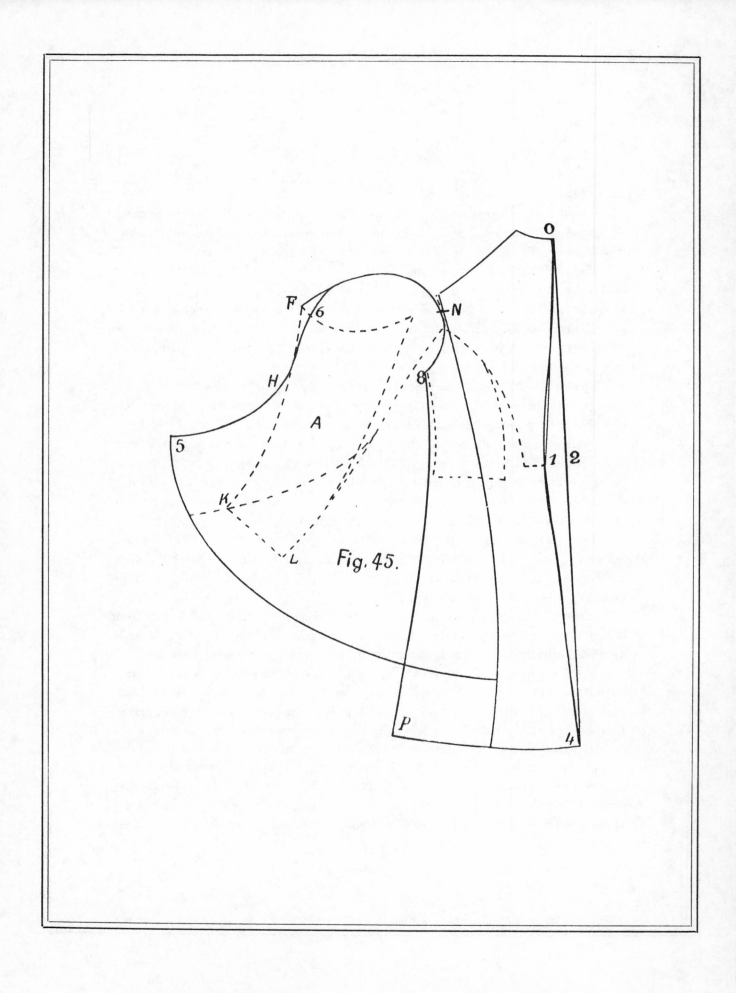

Fig. 45.

from **C** up to 10 add ½ inch, and draw the shoulder from 10 to nothing at **D**. Draw ½ inch outside of **H** to top of front, leaving the straight line from **H** downwards, the front line of dolman.

On the side add ½ inch at **E**. Now place the hip measure from the front to **N** on side, deducting the width of back, but adding 2 inches more for ease and fix point **N**. From **E** ½ inch along front pattern draw a line curving out through **N** down to **B**.

Apply the back at **E** to get the length. Then from **C** shoulder point as pivot, sweep from **B** to **A** the bottom line. Also apply the back on shoulder, and regulate by it the front shoulder at **D**.

When a closer garment is wanted, having more shape at side, then the side-seams of the back and the front are curved inward about ¼ inch each, and a cut is put in also under the arm, which suppresses the extra fullness above the hips. When the pattern is drafted, the arm-hole is also pared out about ½ inch lower.

On diag. 44 a line is drawn and the sleeve laid down 1½ inch from 5, and 5 inches from **0**. Then trace along the round top of sleeve. When the shoulder has been made narrower, add over the top of sleeve the same amount taken off shoulder, and lower below what scye has been dropped.

The front of sleeve seam is curved out from the pattern at point **1** 3 inches. This is done, that it may not wrinkle much at inside of arm-seam, when the arms are crooked up or while being carried in a muff. This peculiarity of dolmans, the crooked sleeve, should be carefully looked at, for only in this way can a good sleeve be produced, one that will hang smooth when arm is bent.

Form the lower part of sleeve in any desired shape. To get the correct length stick a pin at centre of sleeve near elbow, and move the bottom of pattern forward to 2. Then make point 2 the same length as the sleeve pattern. This sleeve is sewed in like any other.

Let us now turn to fig. 45. This diagram shows the sleeve attached to the back, and giving a step further in the construction of dolmans.

When the back has been drafted as by our previous explanations, then lay the pattern of the sleeve against it, so that the notch on it will be on the notch of the back, and place a pin at notch to hold it in place. Then swing it forward, or back as it should be to produce the right quantity of fullness wanted.

It will give a loose sleeve when it lays in such a position that the back seam is close to 8, and any distance farther away from point 8, will give a larger fullness.

A close sleeve will be produced when it is swung back so far that the seam overlaps 8 more or less. The farthest point of closeness would be when it covers point 8 one inch. Whatever size is desired, the subsequent drafting is the same.

Now trace along the top from **N** to **F**, and down to the middle of forearm seams. Remove the pin at notch without disturbing the position of the sleeve, and stick it at the centre, point **A**, opposite the elbow, then swing the sleeve forward toward 5 so far that it gives the shape of the arm, crooked as it is when held up in a muff. This will swing upwards from **K** 5 inches.

Now mark the front seam from **H** to 5, and fix the length of the sleeve-pattern at 5. Then by the shoulder point of back, sweep from 5 to the back at **I**, or make the lower part of the sleeve any shape called for.

The front, fig. 46, is produced the same as diag. 43. It shows further how the sleeve is put in, the front point 1 is sewed in at **J**, which latter is the front of one-half of the armhole. It will thus give the regular amount of fullness to be laid over the sleeve-head.

The lower sleeve is cut by the pattern, along the front from 1 to 4, and along the arm-hole from 1 to 6 to within 3 inches of **N**, and this is sewed in like any other sleeve. Then cut it from 6 down to 5, and curve over from 5 to 4.

Of course it is evident the line from 6 to 5 remain loose, which gives play to the movement of the arms.

We now come to fig. 47 for a further illustration. This figure being drafted by the explanations thus far given, and the sleeve being designed, we now will draft the French back. This is done by starting from **F**, curving a line to blade, thence to 2 at waist, which is about 2 inches from the back line to blade, thence to 2 at waist, which is about 2 inches from the back pattern, and making the whole width 4 to 5 inches. From 2 we curve outward toward **Q** and **I** at bottom. The distance between **C** and **I** is made 5 or 6 inches.

Notch point **G** where it goes on to **F**. Curve upper part of sleeve from **G** to 6 and **J**, above the sleeve pattern to match the narrower back, and begin to flatten it at 6, going inside of pattern fully 1 inch at **J**, where a dot is made. From **J** draw to inside elbow, and front of sleeve at **L**. On this diagram point **L** is represented too low down (a fault of the engraver). It should, to give the correct shape, be 2 inches above where it is drawn.

The front being drafted by the same process as diag. 43, we will now change

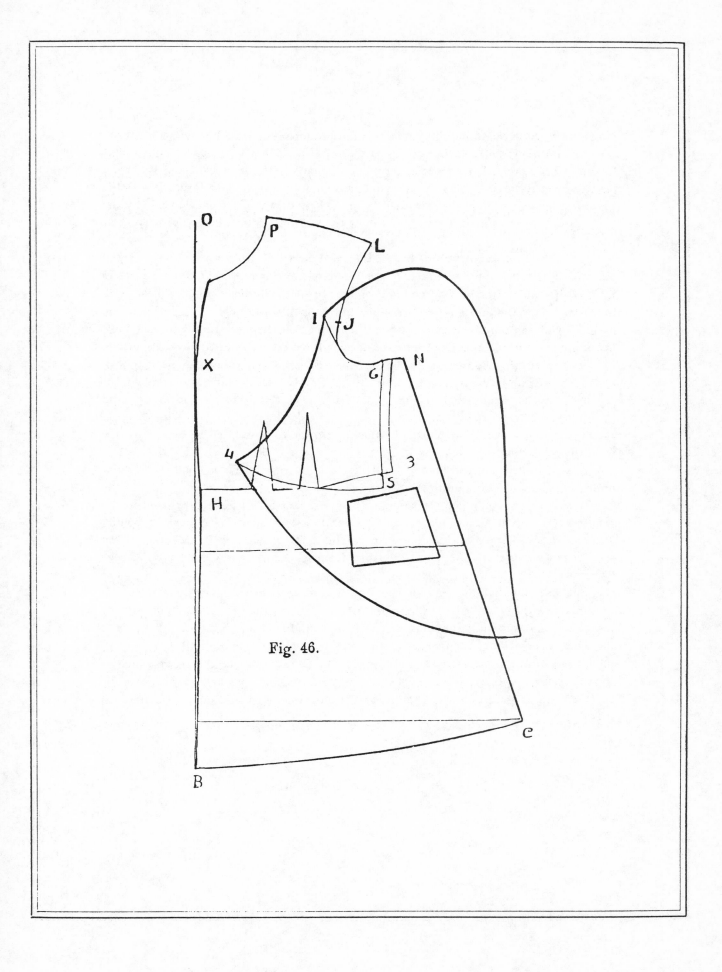

Fig. 46.

it to a different style, in harmony with the back and sleeve of fig. 47, by first drawing the curved line from D which is made as narrow as shoulder to fit the back to S. Point S is the front notch where sleeve is sewed in. From S draft down to K and V; or we can make yet a larger opening for the arm-hole, and draw it from K to R and Q. But it should never be cut below the waist-line for a close fit, for the front must hold the back in the form, while if it is cut out below the waist, there is nothing to keep it at waist.

When the back is cut from Q to I, it is clear the extra width cut away, which is the piece R, D, Q and I, must be added to the front, where it is represented by the letters R, D, B, Q, which in fact represents the side-body. This is then cut in one piece with the front, when the goods is wide enough, but in cutting a large or long garment the material will be found too narrow, when it is better that the piece be cut from R to B, making a straight seam, in preference to adding a three-cornered wheelpiece at bottom.

Before cutting the pattern by the last lines drawn, let us retain the piece at S, E and V, till the under sleeve has been drafted. This is best done by laying the front against the back closing at P (see fig. 49), and at bottom N. Put a weight on it to hold it in place.

The lower sleeve being drafted by the description as illustrated on fig. 46, we lay it on the scye, touching at A and P.

In sewing it in the arm-hole, point H goes on to A, point C to D and the regular under sleeve from C goes on to P.

In producing the under sleeve to fit the arm-hole cut out fig. 48, lay it on to the arm-hole resting on A and P. In order to do this, the upper sleeve must be swung back, till A and H are both together, this will bring under sleeve to P. Then mark on the sleeve the same run of seam as the front, from A, D to F, and cut the lower sleeve like it.

But in order that the seam of the front of sleeve will not show directly on top of arm, it should be pulled over more towards the under side. This is simply done by taking of the lower sleeve about 1 inch at F, and gradually nothing to A. Last raise the upper sleeve above the front, and put in a pin at A, and one on under sleeve at F, then notice if the front seam turns inwards sufficiently to hide the seam, which it should do, by the lower sleeve being short at point P, if it does not, more should be taken off till it gains the right shape, or if it pulls too much, add on a little more till it is right.

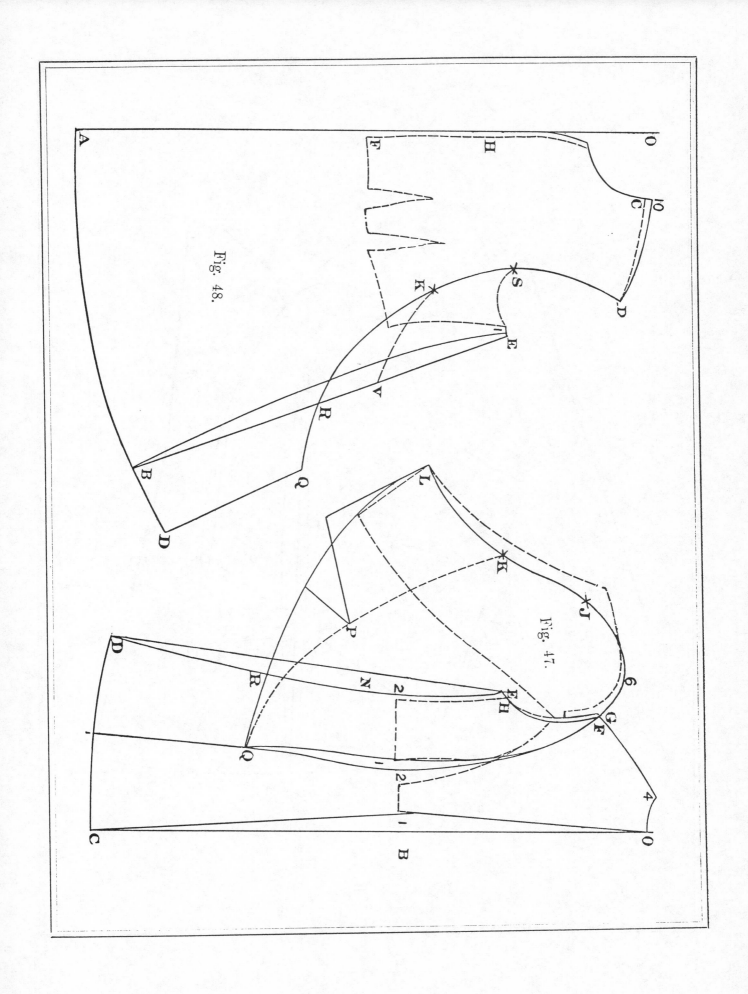

Fig. 48.

Fig. 47.

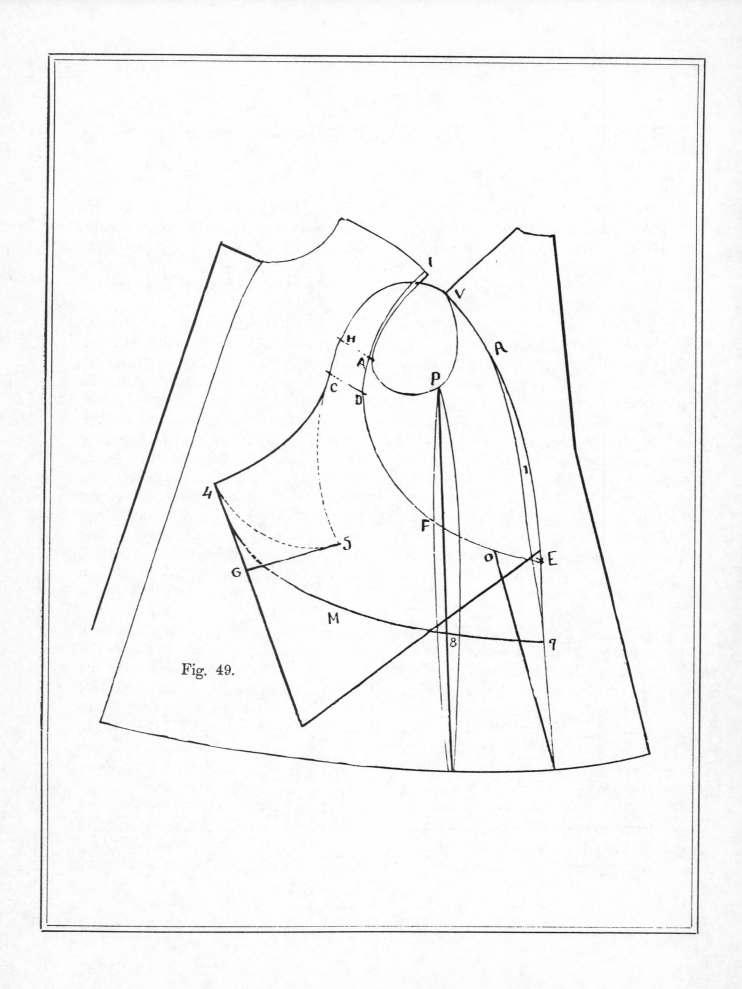

Fig. 49.

THE GILDED AGE

The Gilded Age was a novel written by Mark Twain and Charles Dudly Warner in 1873. The title has come to be used to designate the 1870's, and by some to designate even the 80's and 90's. *The Oxford History of the American People* states: "Mark Twain called it the Gilded Age and when the gilt wore off the brass was left and everyone was trying to make a fast buck". This same work also says: "The Gilded Age was the most lawless and picturesque that America has ever known."

The similarities between the 1870's/early 1880's and recent history are too strong to be overlooked. This was the age of big business and mergers, the Standard Oil Trust, Carnegie Steel, the expansion of major railroads (assisted by Federal grants). Russia had moved into Afghanistan with a view to reaching the ocean in the south and establishing ice-free ports. Thousands of people left the farms and moved to big cities where they could find work. There was a very wide division between the rich and the poor; and in fact this period was known for both the grandiose homes of the very wealthy and the rise of the tenements. Women were moving into the work force in large numbers at all levels. There were arguments about teaching the Bible in schools. It was an age of false morality with a religious veneer on one hand and rampant prostitution on the other. Corruption in goverment was one of the big issues of the time. Many abuses were allowed because people did not want an increase in the power of the Federal government – "that government is best which governs least". There had been a number of Republican administrations, none of them without scandal, and, in fact, Hayes lost the popular vote to Tilden in 1876 but was proclaimed President by Congress anyway.

Some of the major events and personalities of the times were the Centennial Celebration in 1876, the invention and growth of the telephone, the growth of the railroads, the introduction of refrigerated cars for moving produce and meat, the growth of electricity, the first phonograph, Darwin and his doctrine of the "survival of the fittest", the Salvation Army, the Temperance Movement, the attempt of labor to organize, the Red Cross, Gilbert & Sullivan productions in the U. S., Sarah Bernhardt, the opening of the Metropolitan Museum of Art, the rise of the big universities, Carnegie Public Libraries, Walt Whitman, Emily Dickinson, and President Garfield's assassination in 1881.

Regarding women in particular, this was an era when women moved into all types of business in great numbers, due in part to the fact that so many men had been killed in the Civil War. This was so widespread that the etiquette books of the day made special reference to what was to be worn by women in business, and of course it is discussed by all the women's journals of the day. This is also the age of the great profusion of paper patterns which put fashionable garments within the reach of nearly all women. Demorest sold 2 million paper patterns per year by 1873, and Butterick was selling 6 million per year by the early 1870's. There were also half a million sewing machines sold per year at this time. There were a number of ready-made garments available in stores in the United States by this time, and Woolworth opened its first store in Lancaster, Pennsylvania, in 1879. It also might be worth noting that Ibsen's *A Doll's House* was first performed in English in Milwaukee in 1882.

The fact that *A Doll's House* was written during this time is significant. This play is still produced and still has much to say about the status of women in marriage and society. In the 1870's, women seem to be in a great number of positions depending upon their financial and social status as well as their education and outlook on life. We find that women were moving into business; they were also in sweat shops, which were prevalent. It is known that prostitution was prevalent on one level, and on the other end of the scale there were the women who established and perpetuated the strait-laced morals and behavior of the times. These morals were reflected in the almost armorlike fashions of the day.

It might be interesting to note in closing that Anthony Comstock was one of the powers of the time. He got a law passed by Congress prohibiting the sending of obscene matter through the mails – specifically, information about preventing conception or inducing abortion. He was later characterized in a cartoon in which he was shown dragging a woman, by the hair, up in front of a judge; the caption reads, "Your honor, this woman gave birth to a naked child."

WOMEN'S COSTUME: 1877 – 1882

By 1870, the hoops and crinolines of the period from 1840 to after the Civil War had pretty much given way to the bustle. This bustle was high in the back and was augmented by padding over the hips. Skirts were drawn to the back, often ending in a train, and were profusely trimmed with bows, ruffles, etc. By the middle of the decade, the bustle had softened and finally dropped to a small 'mattress' behind the knees, or a supporting petticoat called a 'plumet', and then started to rise again when finally in 1883 it appeared as a saddle-like arrangement that was to persist throughout much of the 1880's.

Mila Contini, in *Fashion: From Ancient Egypt to the Present Day*, has a very interesting discussion about the bustle: "The 'pouf', or small saddle, which shaped the bustle consisted of a horsehair cushion or one or two starched frills, but later developed into an actual support composed of several hoops in the shape of a horseshoe, held in place horizontally by laces or bands. This was suspended like a cage between the skirt and the underskirt at the back. Over this cage the material of the dress would be draped." She goes on to compare the line and drapery of dresses to the drapery of the curtains of the period.

During this time too the bodices, or upper part of the dresses, were very tailored with high necklines and long sleeves, and stiffened with bones. In its most severe form this bodice, also called a cuirass bodice, extended down to points both in the front and the back and it curved up over the hips like a suit of armor. Hecklinger deals with this by providing a pattern for a 'body-waist or dress-waist' (fig. 10), then a 'large size draft' for heavier women (fig. 11), and finally for a 'body-waist lengthened below the waist-line' (fig. 12) for which he gives two different shapes at the bottom – one of which is very pointed (a cuirass bodice) and was very well suited to some forms of the polonaise dress, and the other more squared off and more suited to be incorporated into the princess line dress. These same three patterns are then used as a basis for several of the outer garments as shown on the pattern drafts.

Fashions seemed to be giving two different messages, much like the political and social values of the day. One one hand clothes were very severe, tailored, and mannish; this took the emphasis away from the bust and the front of the dress and at the same time gave women much more freedom of movement. This might well have reflected the fact that many women were active in business and were becoming greatly interested in such sports as cycling, tennis, croquet, skating, golf, and riding. On the other hand clothes were highly decorated with lots of frills, puffs, bows, feathers and laces, and women carried parasols and fans, wore dainty hats and lots of jewelry; the emphasis was directed to the back of the dress – to the bustle and the decorations. This might have reflected the fact that women were considered 'objects' by most men and by society in general.

Probably no garment reflected this double standard more than the princess style dress which was graceful, elaborate, feminine, and very tailored. Ella Church says of it: "The prettiest and most graceful of dresses is the garment known as the Duchesse, or Princess dress, in which the waist and skirt are of one piece, like a long-continued basque – giving an easy flowing air to the figure, instead of cutting it up into sections. Its very simplicity is a work of art, and depends for effect upon the perfect fit and stylish cut of the dress." (This quote shows us why tailors became so interested in women's garments at this time.) The princess style, which actually originated in the 1840's and survived well into the 1930's and 40's in varying forms, was extremely popular in the late 1870's and early 80's when it was associated with the Princess of Wales. We must remember that Queen Victoria remained in seclusion for many years after the death of Prince Albert and embodied the principal reason why there was so much emphasis on mourning and mourning dress during the Victorian era. Thus, the Prince and Princess of Wales, later King Edward VII and Queen Alexandra, became the arbiters of fashion at this time. The basic cut of the princess style dress is in panels from the bottom of the gored skirt to the neckline with no waistline seam, with the body shaping in the area of the torso achieved by means of vertical darts in the seams.

In looking at the princess style pattern it is also well to realise that it can have other possibilities by using different types of materials and making some slight alterations. Ella Church says: "Very pretty morning dresses, as well as dressing-gowns and wrappers, are made from the Princess pattern; and the only alteration needed is to make it rather looser, particularly at the waist. The Watteau fold is especially suitable and becoming for a garment of this character." The Watteau fold or back was made with deep box pleats which go from the neckline to the hem. This is also called a sack back.

Sometimes the princess style was combined with a polonaise to form a princess polonaise dress. Ella Church says: "The Princess polonaise is merely a Princess dress gathered up at the back, or the widths (some cut larger than the others) plaited into each other; arranged, in fact, in any style, the basis of the cut of the garment always the same." The polonaise dress had an overskirt which could be open in the front from the waist down, or not; in any case, it was pulled up and to the back to expose the underskirt. The skirt for a polonaise dress could either be princess style or not and the top or bodice could be any of the three given. Underskirts worn with this type dress were often trained and decorated. The balmoral skirt, *i.e.*, petticoat, was one of the types worn under this dress.

Another type of dress worn at this time was the 'tunic' dress, comprised of an overskirt, an underskirt, and a tight fitting bodice. The overskirt was pulled up decorously to expose the underskirt. These dresses fell in a straighter line than the princess style dress and were without a train. They were worn for informal occasions and for sportwear. In time as a more dressy version of the tunic dress came to be worn, this, and the polonaise, came to mean the same thing. Ella Church says: "The trimming of skirts varies greatly; crosswise bands or folds, gathered and plaited ruffles, and flounces are the principal styles, and sometimes these are all combined on one garment. For gathered ruffles, a quarter of a yard extra to every yard is the proper allowance for fullness; and in plaitings which touch [each other], box-, knife-, or kilt-plaiting three times the length around the skirt is necessary. When more or less plain space is left between the plaits, the amount may be scanted accordingly. For upper or over-skirts, fashion is so capricious that no measures can be given. Sometimes short and sometimes long, 'to one thing constant never,' . . . Little or no trimming is used on the over-skirt, even in handsome materials; and, situated as it is between basque and skirt very little is needed." These same comments can apply to all the skirts worn at this time. Some of these draperies were caught up with bows, fringe, and/or balls of steel or jet.

A tunic or a blouse was also a loose garment used for household duties and for some sports; at times this is also referred to as a sacque. Naomi Tarrant mentions that even the fashion publications of the day (naming the Lady Dressmaker as an example) were confused about fashion nomenclature in this regard.

In a more general sense there is a discussion of clothes in the reprint of the Lord & Taylor catalogue which says that they were anti-anatomical, and that even in evening dresses the figure was clothed from throat to toe, that the contours of the bust and waist were so padded and boned that they conformed to the bodice rather than the other way around.

The 'aesthetic' dress was an attempt at this time to reform dress as a protest by a small group of people in England against corsets and tight bodices. The dress was a very loose, free flowing garment derived from the 14th century smock. It had a high waist and puffed sleeves, appeared to be very limp and lank, and usually was of very subdued colors. This was satirised both in *Punch* by Du Maurier and in *Patience* by Gilbert and Sullivan. This style did not catch on in the United States. However, the dress reform movement in Germany did have a great and lasting effect on fashion in the United States in the form of woollen underwear. Jaeger & Co. introduced fine woollen underwear in the form of the union-suit for men and fine woollen underwear for women, especially the 'combination' (*i.e.*, the chemise and drawers combined). Women also wore woollen stockings at this time, usually of merino.

There was a great upsurge of fashion interest during the period. This was brought about in part because of the United States Centennial Exposition in Philadelphia in 1876, at which there was a Woman's Pavilion as well as a Demorest display in the main building, and the Historical Exhibition of Costume of France which was held in 1878. The French exhibition featured historical garments and accessories from the Middle Ages to the present time. These were augmented by the loan of a number of costumes from the Scandinavian Ethnological Museum of Stockholm. Katherine Lester says: "This was a wonderful collection and proved a great incentive to manufacturers, designers, milliners, and all concerned with the production of beautiful wearing apparel." This helped lead to a fashion-conscious public who were very particular about what they wore and when they wore it.

But not all women could afford one dress for this occasion and another for that, multiplied many times, so many of the dresses could be adapted. In fact, frequently there was a way to button an overskirt on to a more simple dress so that it would be suitable for fancier occasions. This concept can be explored further by referring to the illustration section: we have presented an illustration from *Peterson's* showing this and have given their instructions on how to make it. Also it was possible to attach a train onto a petticoat so that it could be worn with a dress that had a train, and even to have a skirt with two possible trains, one for the house and one for more formal wear outside of the home. In looking through the section in "The Etiquette of Dress" which describes a woman's basic trousseau, it soon becomes obvious that women were expected to have a profusion of clothes. This basic trousseau does not even take into account the clothes that were needed for special occasions as shown in the other sections.

Ready-to-wear was becoming increasingly available in the United States, far more so than in England or Europe. In part this is an outgrowth of the industry that grew up around the textile mills during the Civil War to produce uniforms, etc. However, good dresses and indeed all the clothes of more well to do women were made by dressmakers. Dressmakers had shops, of course, and there were dressmaking departments in the department stores. Dressmakers also went to the homes of some of their customers and some women hired seamstresses who would work in the house for a period of time every year doing the necessary sewing. Also, there were many women who made their own clothes.

A half-million sewing machines were being sold per year in the 1870's. But Ella Church says: "The sewing-machine, though undoubtedly a great gain as a labor-saving invention, has much of this to answer for. Like a willing servant, more is expected of it than it is able to perform. 'Just run it up on the machine' is a direction that does not apply with equally good results to all kinds of sewing; and the habit is apt to produce a careless style of working. Then, too, the finishing off of a work after the machine has done its duty is quite an important item . . ."

The Lady's Maid; Her Duties and How to Perform Them, says of hand-sewing; "It will be advantageous to you if you happen to like plain-work; for the making as well as the mending of your lady's linen [under-garments] will be one of your employments while you are in training. Some people like doing plain-work better than dress-making and millinery; and I think there is something pleasant in the regular work of doing a long seam or hem without stirring from one's chair; or perhaps two in the course of the morning." And it says of the sewing machine: "I have said that they have their advantages as well as disadvantages. Of the former the chief, perhaps, is that with a sewing-machine a great deal of work can be done very quickly, while among the latter, unless you have a lock-stitch, the greatest, possibly, is that when a stitch gives way the safety of the entire seam is placed in jeopardy. There can be no doubt whatever that for all kinds of plain-work in which strength and durability are essential, hand-sewing with the old-fashioned needle is preferable, while for putting on an elaborate mass of braiding which one often sees now-a-days on summer dresses, and winter dresses too, for that matter, or for doing anything in the way of needlework in which despatch is required, the sewing-machine may be called to one's assistance with obvious advantage."

The greatest boost to fashion was the sized tissue paper pattern. Demorest claims to have started tissue paper patterns, but most historians believe that these were started by Butterick, who were certainly the leaders in the field. The account given in *The Delineator*, November, 1910, is that one day Ellen Butterick modestly proposed that a paper pattern for a child's dress might be a boon to mothers. The idea developed, resulting in a drafted and cut pattern for a child's Garibaldi suit [a two-piece suit: collarless, dropped-shoulder blouse plus trousers for boys or skirts for girls, both trimmed with binding or rickrack; inspired by the clothes of the Italian patriot Giuseppe Garibaldi, and popular in the 1860's], which was the first paper pattern offered to the world . . . Then came the desire for women's patterns. In 1871, over six million paper patterns were sold [by Butterick]. Demorest had an office in Paris and Butterick had one in London. Just as they brought the latest fashions directly to the women of the United States, they also in turn influenced fashions through their paper patterns which were sold in England, Canada, Australia and probably Europe as well. A specific instance of this is that in 1878 Demorest promoted skirts that cleared the ground; the idea did catch on and the fashion changed.

Prior to this time, all the skirts dragged on the ground and many references were made in the etiquette books to the fact that ladies should not allow their skirts to drag in the mud and filth of the streets. Eileen Collard says: "An attempt to control them resulted in the invention of the dress suspender; but most women clutched the excess length in their hands." This dress suspender was probably what is called a 'dress holder', a device made with two pendant chains ending in clips which was in use in the 1870's. Naomi Tarrant mentions a wedding dress: "The skirt has a cord down each side of the train ending in buttons on the waistband, which, when pulled, raise the train"; and another: "a long cord loop on the train to hold it up". Skirts were worn with a 'balayeuse', which was a removable and washable dust ruffle basted under the skirt hemline. It was this sort of thing that Demorest was trying to get away from and they succeeded in part. However, the more formal dresses continued to be long and have trains.

Sleeves in this period were either full length or three-quarter length for all but formal ball-gowns. Frilled or lace collars and cuffs were attached either directly to the dress or to the undergarments; these could be detached and laundered and/or could be replaced with others of a different style.

Cutting books and tailoring systems, in general, do not give a lot of detail regarding the actual making up and decoration of garments. This book is no exception. Figure #1 on page 13 illustrates this point very well. Notice the tapes holding the dress fullness to the back, the bow in the back and the other gathering details, as well as all the decoration at the front of the skirt. The author presumes that dressmakers fully understand the fashions of the day and how to individualize each dress to the client's wishes. Naomi Tarrant, in *Great Grandmother's Clothes*, is very enlightening about this as she has a large section on the structure of dresses. She talks about the tapes which were sewn into the seams and used to pull the fullness of the skirt to the back; sometimes elastic ties were also used for this. Often, steels were inserted into horizontal channels in the back of the skirt to make it puff out. It is exceedingly helpful that in the description of each dress illustrated she notes what construction elements were found in the garment. Examples of this are: "Trained princess line wedding dress of ivory satin heavily trimmed with gauging [trim, discussed below]. The bodice has nine bones and a 21½ inch waist. The skirt fullness is controlled by a pair of ties below the waist and a drawstring at the ankle [this was used to draw the front of the dress flat, and almost hobbled the wearer]. Applied pocket on the right hip. 1881."; and "Evening dress of pale blue silk trimmed with cream blonde machine-made lace, embroidered net and pale lavender corded silk ribbon. 26 inch waist, four bones in the bodice and bust pads [used to fill the shoulder hollows and present a smooth, full front]. Bodice edge weighted with lead weights. Detachable D-shaped train. About 1882."

The skirts were sheath-like and flat in front and could be very plain or highly decorated. Eileen Collard says: "Fashionable skirts had frilled flouncing, decorative strappings, bows, knots, rouleaus, cords and jet beaded tassels stitched through the dress material to the fitted under-skirt." One of the decorative elements was gauging, which was a type of shirring or a series of close parallel running stitches so that the material in between is fixed in gathers, somewhat like smocking before the decorative stitches are added in its simplest form. It could also be much more elaborately gathered into ruching.

There are a number of sources which can be investigated for construction stitches and techniques, and for the more decorative stitches used for the clothes of this period:

Butterick. *The Dressmaker*, both the 1911 first edition and the 1916 revised edition. New York. Edwardian dressmaking books, but they show the construction needed to make garments of the Victorian period. This includes putting bones in garments and making a large number of ornamental trims, a dust ruffle, and construction techniques.

Carens, Edith. *Dressmaking Self Taught*, 1911. Jacksonville. A small book on dressmaking in 24 lessons; Edwardian, but applicable to some Victorian techniques. This book is not very well illustrated, but it is a guide, especially to machine sewing.

Caufield, S. F. & Blanche Saward. *Encyclopedia of Victorian Needlework*, 1882/revised 1886. Republished in 1985 in two volumes by Dover. New York. There is a lot of construction information but it has to be sorted out of the general needlework.

Collard, Eileen (ed.) *Robertson & Bros Guide to Dressmaking and Fancy Work*, ca. 1875. Republished 1977 by Collard. Burlington, Ontario. Some good information, but here again it supposes you know more than you might. Illustrated with dress patterns, but not tailored garments, plus underwear patterns, stitches, ornamental trims, and fashions.

Frost, S. Annie. *The Ladies' Guide to Needle Work*, 1877. Republished 1987 by R. L. Shep. Lopez Island. No information on construction but it does show the fancy stitches needed for trim and decoration, such as braiding, fringe, embroidery, lace, beadwork, etc. It also illustrates and gives instructions for making many fashion accessories for this period, including purses, travelling cases, baskets, etc.

Undergarments have been discussed in terms of the wearing of wool and the introduction of the 'combination'. There is more information about what was worn and when, in "The Etiquette of Dress". There are a few additional things worth noting dealing with the arrangements women made for wearing petticoats. The 'Petticoat-supporter Corset' and the 'waist which served as a skirt-supporter' (it must be noted that "skirt" in this case is a euphemism for "petticoat", a word which Mrs. Duffey would not write; she also used "stays" for the word "corset") both had a row of buttons near the bottom on which the petticoats could be hung. This did away with bulk around the waist and hips; it also put the weight of these garments onto the shoulders. Eileen Collard shows yet another item called a 'petticoat-band' which she says was "an almost semi-circular yoke to which the narrow band of a new styled petticoat (which did not come up to the waistline) could be fastened to it by buttonholes or tape loops" (*sic*). Many petticoats had a row of ruffles or flounces down the back to take the place of the bustle and make the back of the dress stay away from the body.

Basically this was a period of profusion of fashion accessories. The best way to get a sense of just what items were being worn, and what they were like, is to look at the fashion illustrations of the period from *Godey's, Peterson's, Harper's Bazar,* or other publications.

Both bonnets and hats were popular; bonnets tied under the chin and hats did not; some of them were fussy and some very plain. The most popular materials for hats and bonnets were straw and felt. The trimmings used might be ribbons, lace, flowers, jewelled pins, feathers, and even whole stuffed birds. A bonnet from the November 5, 1881, issue of *Harper's Bazar* is described as being a black straw with red roses, black plume, black satin ribbon ties, and jet ornament on crown. At the same time, some women were wearing very plain hats, as evidenced from figures 4 and 5 on pages 18 and 19. Women also wore caps such as night caps, morning caps, etc., which had ribbons, streamers, lace, and so forth.

Whole stuffed birds also appeared on fans, as did other feathers, lace, ivory, silk, muslin, spangles, etc. Fans were universally used both in the daytime and in the evening and came in a large variety of shapes and sizes. It was said that no toilette could be complete without one.

Handkerchiefs, usually white with embroidery, were used for general occasions, and a fancier handkerchief trimmed with lace was used for dress occasions.

Parasols were indispensible during the summer and were often made of lace and had very decorative handles; umbrellas were often used in winter, although Mrs. Duffey states that a waterproof with a hood was preferable.

Aprons were often worn at home, and of course they are an essential feature of the dress of any domestic worker such as housekeeper, maid, cook, or seamstress. They seemed to be worn as a fashionable item of clothing in England, but there is little evidence that they ever caught on in this sense in the United States.

Gloves were essential whether of kid, Lisle thread, suede, or wash-leather, different types being worn for different occasions as outlined in "The Etiquette of Dress". And muffs were worn for warmth during the winter. Dresses often had pockets, both for handkerchiefs and for watches, but outer garments did not; therefore, very small handbags were often used.

Both shoes and boots, especially of kid, were worn although boots were definitely worn during the winter. The Lord & Taylor catalogue for 1881 shows far more boots than it does shoes. Boots had fairly pointed toes, short concave heels and buttons on the side. There are a few low shoes which look like cut-off boots. There are also a few ladies' slippers, which look like pumps with the same type of concave heel.

The jewelry of the late 1870's and early 1880's tended to be fairly heavy and large. Mrs. Duffey mentions brooches and the indispensible watch and chain for the business woman. As she also talks about not wearing jewels and glittering gems at inappropriate times, we can only suppose that many women did! Jet and onyx were used extensively, and were especially worn for mourning.

There certainly was a wide range of jackets, coats, mantles, and cloaks available at this time. There does seem to be a confusion in terminology not only between one source and another but often within the same source. The Lord & Taylor catalogue for 1881 shows the following under the heading of "Cloaks": dolman-ulster, Ulster, walking-coat, walking-jacket, dolman, cape. They are all different one from the other and very few look like what we would term a cloak. It is also sometimes difficult to determine just what is being presented in Hecklinger; we have tried to combat this problem by defining each garment in the glossary.

Both the 1870's and 1880's were known as the age of the mantle, which is a cape or cloak (a longer form), with or without sleeves. The dolman is a mantle with a sleeve made as a part of the side piece and hanging loose. The dolman was very popular during this period and changed only in whether the back had to accommodate a bustle. Dolman sleeves restricted the movement of the arms and thus dolmans were used for a more decorative effect than were coats. Dolmans were often made of cashmere or satin and highly trimmed with lace, ribbons, braid, silk and/or bead fringe. Some dolmans had hoods lined with silk or satin.

The coats of the period (surtout, long oversack or Ulster, and loose oversack) were used more for active and practical activities such as travelling, skating, raincoats or waterproofs, etc. These were made of more durable fabrics like wool, tweed, or alpaca, and were trimmed with braid and fancy buttons.

Paisley shawls were still worn and some of the older ones were cut up and made into mantles.

There were even more decorative mantles like the Talma which were long and usually worn with evening dress. Hecklinger refers to them as wraps; they could be made with or without sleeves, and they could serve as an opera wrap. The Talma was named for a famous French actor of the Consulate and Empire periods.

Along with these there were short jackets which were more form fitting and followed the lines of the bodice of the dress. They were made of various materials, depending upon where they were to be worn, from heavy wool to plush and velvet, and often trimmed with fur, decorated with braid and/or jet beads. Jackets and coats made entirely of fur became fashionable in the late 1870's.

Naomi Tarrant says that the basic form of both the mantle and the coat did not really change during the period and persisted until the end of the 1880's. These patterns can be used with slight variations for the 1870's and 1880's.

There were many things that were worn for special occasions, when going to special places, for weddings, for mourning, etc. These are all discussed extensively in "The Etiquette of Dress", both in terms of what was proper to wear and in terms of what materials and color they should be.

In the illustrations that follow, we have tried to present a range of garments worn between the years 1877 and 1882. These are primarily illustrations from American sources. The exception might be seen in the illustrations from *Der Bazar*, but not really. *Der Bazar* and *Harper's Bazar* were essentially the same publication, one being in German and the other in English, sharing illustrations, so we have used what was available. Also, we have presented these illustrations without comment, other than source and date identification, leaving them as a research resource for the reader to use as needed. We have tried to include multiple examples of the same type garment from pattern catalogues to give an idea of some of the variations that are possible. And in keeping with the nature of this book we have tried to present as many outer garments, dolmans, wraps, coats, etc., as possible.

Both illustrations from
Harper's Bazar, Jan. 1877

Der Bazar, August 1880

Der Bazar, April 1880

Dress with Attachable Over-Skirt
Peterson's August 1879

"Our model has first a foundation for the front and side gores of the skirt, on to which two knife-plaitings are arranged. Over this the material is placed, cut out in deep vandykes. Then the tunic and paniers are made and adjusted to this under foundation: trimmed to correspond, with knife-plaiting on the front, and the back of the short demi-train is simply bound. The looping is arranged by strings underneath. The basque is cut straight in front, and the back is cut in two vandykes, half-way below the waistline, where it is filled in with fine knife-plaitings to correspond with the skirt. Cuffs, collars, pockets, bindings, are all in a solid colored cambric, to correspond with the other part of the dress, or else of a contrasting color. This costume may be made with a short, round skirt for walking, and the tunic adjusted all the same. For the latter, make the trimming for the bottom of the skirt, the same all around, and the back of the tunic shorter. Fourteen to fifteen yards of material."

Wool Dress
Der Bazar
Sept. 1880

5154

Lady's Surtout Wrapper
(indoor wear)
Smith's Pattern Bazaar
1880

Flannel Wrapper
Harper's Bazaar
Jan. 1877

Under-dress
Harper's Bazar, Sept. 1879

Muslin Drawers
Harper's Bazar, Sept. 1878

Button-on Train for Petticoat
Der Bazar, Aug. 1880

Chemise
Harper's Bazar, Sept. 1878

Combination
Smith's Pattern Bazaar, 1880

Skirt with two trains; one for Home, one for Street
(The trains button on)
Smith's Pattern Bazaar, 1880

2023   Ladies' Basque. 9 Sizes. 30 to 46 inches, Bust Measure. Price, 25 cents.

Cat. "Domestic Fashions", Fall 1880

FIGURE No. 5.—LADIES' DRESSING SACK.

The Delineator, Aug. 1881

2026   Ladies' Basque. 9 Sizes. 30 to 46 inches, Bust Measure. Price, 25 cents.

Cat. "Domestic Fashions", Fall 1880

Night-cap
Harper's Bazar, Sept. 1878

Waterproofed Rain Coat.
Der Bazar. Sept. 1880

2022 - Catalogue of Domestic Fashion, Fall 1880

502 - Smith's Pattern Bazaar, Summer 1880
(lower left) Mantles. Der Bazar, Sept. 1880

2022 Ladies' Basque. 9 Sizes.
30 to 46 inches, Bust Measure.
Price, 25 cents.

502

1970 Ladies' Mantle.
9 Sizes. 30 to 46 inches.
Price, 25 cents.

Cat. "Domestic Fashions", Fall 1880

2031 Ladies' Dolman.
9 Sizes. 30 to 46 inches, Bust Measure.
Price, 30 cents.

Cat. "Domestic Fashions", Fall 1880

2021 Ladies' Dolman, 9 Sizes.
30 to 46 inch., Bust Meas.
Price, 30 cents.

Cat. "Domestic Fashions", Fall 1880

Dolmans
Peterson's, Nov. 1879

Fig. 1.—Olive Green Velvet Bonnet.   Fig. 2.—Brown Felt Bonnet.—Front.   Fig. 3.—Brown Felt Bonnet.—Back.

Sept. 1877

7659

Front View.

LADIES' POLONAISE.

7659

Back View.

The Delineator, Aug. 1881

**Woman Dressed for Sports (Tennis)
The Delineator, Aug. 1881**

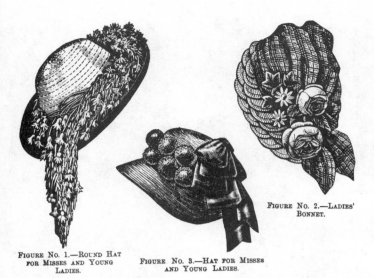

FIGURE NO. 1.—ROUND HAT FOR MISSES AND YOUNG LADIES.

FIGURE NO. 3.—HAT FOR MISSES AND YOUNG LADIES.

FIGURE NO. 2.—LADIES' BONNET.

**Hat
Peterson's, Nov. 1879**

FIGURE NO. 4.—LADIES' HAT.

FIGURE NO. 5.—LADIES' ROUGH-AND-READY STRAW HAT.

The Delineator, August 1881

**Morning-cap
Der Bazar, Aug. 1880**

FIGURE NO. 6.—LADIES' POKE BONNET.

FIGURE NO. 7.—LADIES' HAT.

FIGURE NO. 8.—LADIES' BONNET.

**Bonnet
Godey's, Sept. 1879**

The Delineator, August 1881

997 Ladies' Waterproof Circular. 9 Sizes. 30 to 46 inches, Bust Measure. Price, 35 cents.

1641 Ladies' Traveling Cloak. 9 Sizes. 30 to 46 inches, Bust Measure. Price, 30 cents.

1364 Ladies' Sacque Cloak. 9 Sizes. 30 to 46 inches, Bust Measure. Price, 30 cents.

37 Ladies' Waterproof. 9 Sizes. 30 to 46 inches, Bust Measure. Price, 35 cents.

1868 Ladies' Cloak. 9 Sizes. 30 to 46 inch., Bust Meas. Price, 30 cents.

1853 Ladies' Reception Dress. 9 Sizes. 30 to 46 inches, Bust Measure. Price, 35 cents.

1841 Ladies' Princesse Dress. 9 Sizes. 30 to 46 in., Bust Measure. Price, 35 cents.

1406 Ladies' Traveling Cloak. 9 Sizes. 30 to 46 inches, Bust Measure. Price, 30 cents.

All illustrations from Catalogue of "Domestic Fashions", Fall 1880

1504 Ladies' Coat. 9 Sizes. 30 to 46 inches, Bust Measure. Price, 25 cents.

1608 Ladies' Coat. 9 Sizes. 30 to 46 in., Bust Meas. Price, 25 cts.

1923 Ladies' Surtout. 9 Sizes. 30 to 46 in., Bust Meas. Price, 30 cents.

1590 Ladies' Coat. 9 Sizes. 30 to 46 inches, Bust Measure. Price, 25 cents.

1421 Ladies' Coat. 9 Sizes. 30 to 46 inches, Bust Measure. Price, 25 cents.

1942 Ladies' Polonaise. 9 Sizes. 30 to 46 inches, Bust Measure. Price, 35 cents.

1855 Ladies' Polonaise. 9 Sizes. 30 to 46 inches, Bust Measure. Price, 35 cents.

1928 Ladies' Polonaise. 9 Sizes. 30 to 46 inches, Bust Measure. Price, 35 cents.

1893 Ladies' Polonaise. 9 Sizes. 30 to 46 inches, Bust Measure. Price, 35 cents.

1933 Ladies' Polonaise. 9 Sizes. 30 to 46 inches, Bust Measure. Price, 35 cents.

SUPPLEMENT FOR MAY, 1879.

6574

6574

6552

6552

6598

6598

6568

6568

6566

6566

6557

6557

6575

6575

6576

6576

6583

6583

Ladies' Draped Princess Dress: 13 sizes. Bust meas. 28 to 46 inches. Any size, 40 cents, or 1s. 8d. St'g.

Ladies' Circular Wrapper: 13 sizes. Bust measures, 28 to 46 inches. Any size, 30 cents, or 1s. 3d. Sterling.

Ladies' Wrapper: 13 sizes. Bust measures, 28 to 46 inches. Any size, 30 cents, or 1s. 3d. St'g.

Ladies' Shirred Princess Dress: 13 sizes. Bust measures, 28 to 46 inches. Any size, 40 cents, or 1s. 8d. Sterling.

Ladies' Polonaise: 13 sizes. Bust measures, 28 to 46 inches. Any size, 35 cents, or 1s. 6d. Sterling.

Misses' Princess Dress: 8 sizes. Ages, 8 to 15 years. Any size, 30 cents, or 1s. 3d. Sterling.

Ladies' Short Walking Dress: 13 sizes. Bust measures, 28 to 46 inches. Any size, 35 cents, or 1s. 6d. Sterling.

Ladies' Polonaise, with Plaited Back Drapery: 13 sizes. Bust measures, 28 to 46 inches. Any size, 35 cents, or 1s. 6d. St'g.

All illustrations from Butterick Summer Catalogue 1879

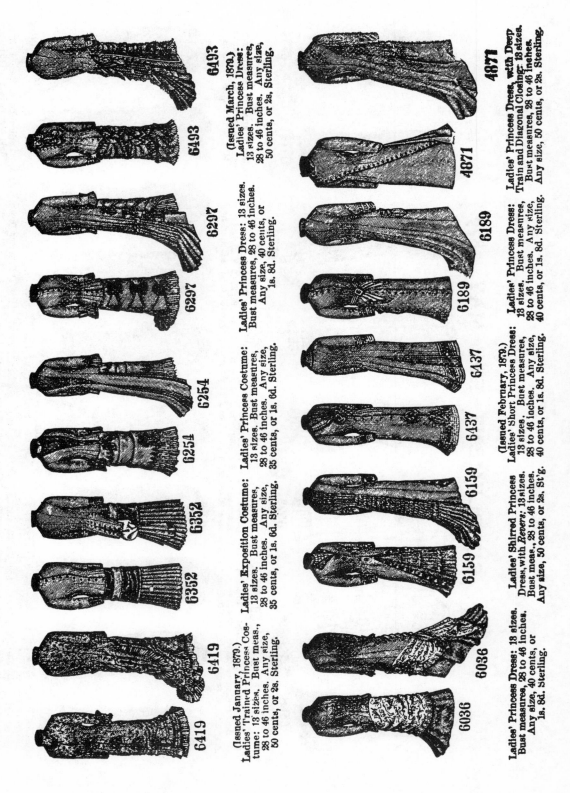

6493 6493

(Issued March, 1879.)
Ladies' Princess Dress:
13 sizes. Bust measures,
28 to 46 inches. Any size,
50 cents, or 2s. Sterling.

4871 4871

Ladies' Princess Dress, with Deep
Train and Diagonal Closing: 13 sizes.
Bust measures, 28 to 46 inches.
Any size, 50 cents, or 2s. Sterling.

6297 6297

Ladies' Princess Costume: 13 sizes.
Bust measures, 28 to 46 inches, or
1s. 8d. Sterling.

6189 6189

Ladies' Princess Dress:
13 sizes. Bust measures,
28 to 46 inches. Any size,
40 cents, or 1s. 8d. Sterling.

6254 6254

Ladies' Exposition Costume:
13 sizes. Bust measures,
28 to 46 inches. Any size,
35 cents, or 1s. 6d. Sterling.

6437 6437

(Issued February, 1879.)
Ladies' Short Princess Dress:
13 sizes. Bust measures,
28 to 46 inches. Any size,
40 cents, or 1s. 8d. Sterling.

6352 6352

(Issued January, 1879.)
Ladies' Trained Princess Costume: 13 sizes. Bust meas.,
28 to 46 inches. Any size,
50 cents, or 2s. Sterling.

6159 6159

Ladies' Shirred Princess
Dress, with *Revers*: 13 sizes.
Bust meas., 28 to 46 inches.
Any size, 50 cents, or 2s. St'g.

6419 6419

Ladies' Princess Dress: 13 sizes.
Bust measures, 28 to 46 inches, or
1s. 8d. Sterling.

6036 6036

Ladies' Princess Dress: 13 sizes.
Bust measures, 40 cents, or
1s. 8d. Sterling.

All illustrations from Butterick Summer Catalogue 1879

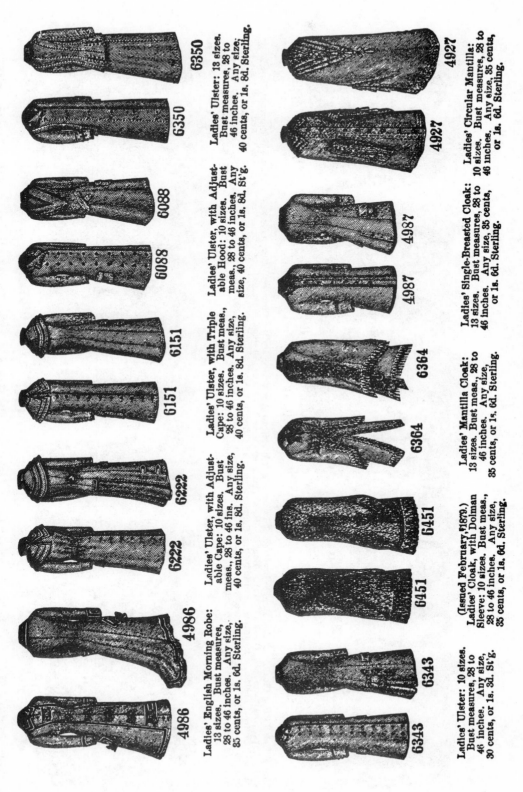

6350

6350

Ladies' Ulster: 13 sizes.
Bust measures, 28 to
46 inches. Any size,
40 cents, or 1s. 8d. Sterling.

6088

6088

Ladies' Ulster, with Adjustable Hood: 10 sizes. Bust meas., 28 to 46 inches. Any size, 40 cents, or 1s. 8d. St'g.

6151

6151

Ladies' Ulster, with Triple Cape: 10 sizes. Bust meas., 28 to 46 inches. Any size, 40 cents, or 1s. 8d. Sterling.

6222

6222

Ladies' Ulster, with Adjustable Cape: 10 sizes. Bust meas., 28 to 46 ins. Any size, 40 cents, or 1s. 8d. Sterling.

4986

4986

Ladies' English Morning Robe:
13 sizes. Bust measures,
28 to 46 inches. Any size,
35 cents, or 1s. 6d. Sterling.

4927

4927

Ladies' Circular Mantilla:
10 sizes. Bust measures, 28 to
46 inches. Any size, 35 cents,
or 1s. 6d. Sterling.

4987

4987

Ladies' Single-Breasted Cloak:
13 sizes. Bust measures, 28 to
46 inches. Any size, 35 cents,
or 1s. 6d. Sterling.

6364

6364

Ladies' Mantilla Cloak:
13 sizes. Bust meas., 28 to
46 inches. Any size,
35 cents, or 1s. 6d. Sterling.

6451

6451

(Issued February, 1879.)
Ladies' Cloak, with Dolman
Sleeve: 10 sizes. Bust meas.,
28 to 46 inches. Any size,
35 cents, or 1s. 6d. Sterling.

6343

6343

Ladies' Ulster: 10 sizes.
Bust measures, 28 to
46 inches. Any size,
30 cents, or 1s. 3d. St'g.

All illustrations from Butterick Summer Catalogue 1879

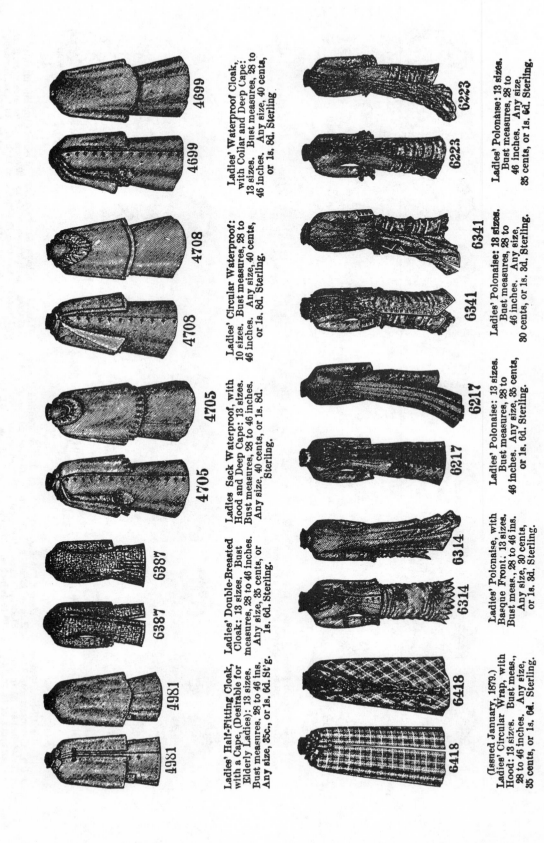

4699   4699

4708   4708

4705   4705

6387   6387

4981   4981

6223   6223

6341   6341

6217   6217

6314   6314

6418   6418

Ladies' Waterproof Cloak, with Collar and Deep Cape: 13 sizes. Bust measures, 28 to 46 inches. Any size, 40 cents, or 1s. 8d. Sterling.

Ladies' Circular Waterproof: 10 sizes. Bust measures, 28 to 46 inches. Any size, 40 cents, or 1s. 8d. Sterling.

Ladies' Sack Waterproof, with Hood and Deep Cape: 13 sizes. Bust measures, 28 to 46 inches. Any size, 40 cents, or 1s. 8d. Sterling.

Ladies' Double-Breasted Cloak: 13 sizes. Bust measures, 28 to 46 inches. Any size, 35 cents, or 1s. 6d. Sterling.

Ladies' Half-Fitting Cloak, with a Cape, (Desirable for Elderly Ladies): 13 sizes. Bust measures, 28 to 46 ins. Any size, 35c., or 1s. 6d. St'g.

(Issued January, 1879.)
Ladies' Circular Wrap, with Hood: 13 sizes. Bust meas., 28 to 46 inches. Any size, 35 cents, or 1s. 6d. Sterling

Ladies' Polonaise: 13 sizes. Bust measures, 28 to 46 inches. Any size, 40 cents, or 1s. 8d. Sterling.

Ladies' Polonaise: 18 sizes. Bust measures, 28 to 46 inches. Any size, 30 cents, or 1s. 3d. Sterling.

Ladies' Polonaise: 13 sizes. Bust measures, 28 to 46 inches. Any size, 35 cents, or 1s. 6d. Sterling.

Ladies' Polonaise, with Basque Front: 13 sizes. Bust meas., 28 to 46 ins. Any size, 30 cents, or 1s. 3d. Sterling.

All illustrations from Butterick Summer Catalogue 1879

THE ETIQUETTE OF DRESS

One of the best ways to find out what was worn in an era is to look at etiquette books of the time. What we present here is a consensus after consulting five such books. All of these books are listed in the bibliography, but the major source is *Ladies' & Gentlemen's Etiquette* by Mrs. E. B. Duffey, Philadelphia, 1877. It is interesting that many of these books repeat word for word exactly the same advice on what to wear even though they are written by different people and often are from different publishers. It is almost as if there really was a "Mrs. Grundy" out there dictating etiquette.

It must also be pointed out that although each of these books pretends to cover etiquette for all classes, it is not really the case. Etiquette books were written for the upper and middle classes and those people who aspired to them. But, on the other hand, the United States is not England and all people could, and did in some measure, aspire to raise themselves up. At least what we have here are guidelines for what should be worn.

FOLLOWING THE FASHIONS IN MODERATION

A sensible woman will not go lank and hoopless when prevailing modes indicate great rotundity of the skirt. She will use garniture moderately when others adopt it profusely; she certainly will not discard it entirely. There is one thing a sensible woman will not do, whatever fashion may insist upon – she will not allow her dress to trail and catch the mud and filth of the street, though all the feminine world pass by her in bedraggled skirts.

The glaring colors, the 'loud' costumes, once so common, have given place to sober grays, and browns, and olives; black predominating over all. Chains of gold, with lockets depending from them, and diamond earrings are no longer worn on the street by those who know what is considered good form in dress.

USING PAINTS

We cannot but allude to the practice of using paints, a habit strongly to be condemned. If for no other reason than that poison lurks beneath every layer, inducing paralytic affections and premature death, they should be discarded – but they are a disguise which deceives no one, even at a distance; there is a ghastly deathliness in the appearance of the skin after it has been painted, which is far removed from the natural hue of health.

EXTRAVAGANCE IN DRESS

Dress, to be in perfect taste, need not be costly. It is unfortunate that in the United States, too much attention is paid to dress by those who have neither the excuse of ample means nor of social culture. The wife of a poorly paid clerk, or of a young man just starting in business aims at dressing as stylishly as does the wealthiest among her acquaintances. The sewing girl, the shop girl, the chambermaid, and even the cook, must have their elegantly trimmed silk dresses and velvet cloaks for Sunday and holiday wear, and the injury done by this state of things to the morals and manners of the poorer classes is incalculable.

LADIES' UNDERCLOTHING

In the matter of underclothing fashion does not rule supreme. Each one is left to suit her own taste and convenience.

A lady's underclothing should always be neatly made, fine, white and scrupulously clean. If there is ornament, let it be delicate rather than showy. A neat row of fine stitching is more indicative of a lady than a multitude of edgings and insertions of imitation lace or cheap embroidery.

Both ladies and gentlemen should wear flannel (*wool flannel next to the body was definitely the order of the day*, ed.) underneath all their other garments, during the winter at least. Some physicians say during the summer also, but that must be optional with the individual. Suitable underwear can be found already made at the furnishing stores.

In ladies' apparel, next to this underwear comes the chemise and drawers, or a garment which is made to do service for both. In some respects the latter garment is preferable to the two separate garments, and is in common use in Europe, while it is being introduced here. It should be made with high neck and long sleeves, and at the neck may be buttons to which fasten the collar or ruff, at the wrists buttons for cuffs. This garment saves the extra clothing around the waist, also the binding of the drawers, which, in order to keep them in their proper place, are apt to be fastened too tightly, and thus sensibly interfere with the functions of the body.

Next to this comes the stays, or if they are not worn a waist which serves as a skirt-supporter. If stays are worn, they should never be laced tightly, should always have shoulder-straps of some sort, and the bones and steels which stiffen them should be few and flexible as possible.

The waist, if adopted instead of stays, should fit the body loosely and have rows of buttons around the waist by which to suspend all the skirts which may be worn, so that their weight shall depend from the shoulders instead of resting upon the hips. This is an important matter; and mothers should see to it that their young daughters' garments are properly arranged in this respect if they would have them escape the illnesses to which women are peculiarly subject. As few skirts should be worn as possible, the required warmth being supplied by added clothing upon the limbs.

APPROPRIATE DRESS

Ladies and gentlemen will always dress accoring to their age, their pecuniary circumstances, the hour of the day, the special occasion and their surroundings. For an old person to assume the light colors and the simplicity of youth is no more incongruous than for the young to put on the richness of dress and abundant jewelry belonging to advanced life.

One does not come down in full dress to breakfast, nor wear a wrapper or shooting-jacket to a ceremonious dinner. One should not go in mourning to a wedding, nor don light color for a funeral. Nor need one in a neighborhood of unusual simplicity appear adorned in the very height of the latest fashions. All these things would be vulgarities and indicate the doer as devoid of good breeding, if not of good sense.

HARMONY OF COLOR IN DRESS

Black not only suits the complexion of all forms, and is becoming to all figures, but is at once piquant and elegant; it has a surprising effect in imparting grace and elegance to a well-turned form.

When two colors which are dissimilar are associated agreeably, such as blue and orange, or lilac and cherry, they form a 'harmony of contrast'. And when two distant tones of one color are associated, such as very light and very dark blue, they harmonize by 'contrast'. Of course, in the latter instance the harmony is neither so striking nor so perfect.

When two colors are grouped which are similar to each other in disposition, such as orange and scarlet, crimson and crimson-brown, or orange and orange-brown, they form a 'harmony of analogy'. And if two or more tones of one color be associated, closely approximating in intensity, they harmonize by 'analogy'.

The harmonies of contrast are more effective, although not more important, than those of analogy; the former are characterized by brilliancy and decision, while the latter are peculiar for their quiet, retiring, and undemonstrative nature. In affairs of dress both hold equal positions; and in arranging colors in costume, care must be taken to adopt the proper species of harmony.

The simplest rules to be observed are the following:

1. When a color is selected which is favorable to the complexion, it is advisable to associate with it tints which will harmonize by analogy, because the adoption of contrasting colors would diminish its favorable effect.

2. When a color is employed in dress which is injurious to the complexion, contrasting colors must be associated with it, as they have the power to neutralize its objectionable influence.

Black hair has its color and depth enhanced by scarlet, orange or white, and will bear diamonds, pearls or lustreless gold.

Dark-brown hair will bear light blue, or dark blue in a lesser quantity.

If the hair has no richness of coloring, a pale, yellowish green will by reflection produce the lacking warm tint.

Light-brown hair requires blue, which sets off to advantage the golden tint.

Pure golden or yellow hair needs blue, and its beauty is also increased by the addition of pearls or white flowers.

Auburn hair, if verging on the red, needs scarlet to tone it down. If of a golden red, blue, green, purple, or black will bring out the richness of its tints.

Flaxen hair requires blue.

MATERIAL FOR DRESS

The material for dress must be selected with reference to the purpose which it is to serve. No one buys a yellow dress for the promenade, yet a yellow satin seen by gaslight is beautiful as an evening-dress. Neither would one buy a heavy serge of neutral tint for an opera-dress.

MORNING-DRESS FOR HOUSE AND STREET

A Lady may appear in a wrapper in the morning, but it should be clean and fresh, and supplemented with spotless collar and cuffs, and with a bright knot of ribbon or bunch of flowers at the throat. No jewelry should be worn at this hour of the day save plain rings, brooch and watch and chain.

MORNING-DRESS FOR HOME

A dress for morning wear at home may be simpler than for visiting or for hotel or boarding-house. A busy housewife will find it desirable to protect her dress with an ample apron. The hair should be plainly arranged, without ornament.

MORNING-DRESS FOR VISITOR

For breakfasting in public or at the house of another the loose wrapper is inadmissible. A dress with a closely-fitting waist must take its place. This for summer may be of cambric, pique, marseilles, or other wash-goods, either white or figured; in winter plain woollen goods, simply made and quietly trimmed, should be adopted.

Breakfast-caps daintily made of lace may be worn, but they must not serve as an excuse for uncombed or carelessly arranged hair.

MORNING-DRESS FOR STREET

The morning-dress for the street should be quiet in color, plainly made and of serviceable material. The dress should be short enough to clear the ground without collecting mud and garbage. White skirts are out of place, the colored ones now found everywhere in furnishing and other stores being much more appropriate.

Jewelry is entirely out of place in any of the semi-business errands which take a lady from her home in the morning. Lisle thread gloves in the summer and cloth ones in winter will be found more serviceable than kid ones. Linen collar and cuffs are more suitable than elaborate neck and wrist dressing. Street walking-boots of kid should be worn.

The bonnet or hat should be quiet and inexpensive, matching the dress as nearly as possible, and displaying no superfluous ornament.

In stormy weather a large waterproof with hood will be found more convenient than an umbrella, which is always troublesome to carry and often difficult to manage.

BUSINESS WOMAN'S DRESS

There are so many women who are engaged in literature, art or business of some sort that it seems really necessary that they should have a distinctive dress suited to their special needs. This dress need not be so peculiar as to mark them out for objects of observation wherever they go, but still it should differ somewhat from the ordinary walking-costume of the sex. Its material should, as a rule, be more serviceable, better fitted to endure the vicissitudes of weather, and of quiet color, such as browns or grays, not easily soiled.

This costume must not be made with quite Quaker-like simplicity, but it should at least dispense with all superfluities in the way of trimming – puffs which crush and crumple, bows which are in the way, and heavy flounces which weigh down the skirt. It ought to be made with special reference to easy locomotion and to the free use of the hands and arms.

Linen cuffs and collar are best suited to this dress, gloves which can be easily removed, street walking-boots and no jewelry save plain cuff-buttons, brooch and the indispensable adjunct of the business woman, a watch and a chain. The hat or bonnet should be neat and pretty, but with few flowers or feathers to be wilted or drooped by the first falling shower.

For winter wear waterproof tastefully made up is the very best material for a business woman's dress.

["Demorest Magazine" noted in 1877 the quiet garb of the professional women as: *A rich black silk with lace served almost as their uniform, they wore high button boots with low heels and carried black fans against somewhat muddy complexions.*]

THE PROMENADE

The dress for the promenade admits of greater richness in material, brilliancy in color and variety in trimming than that of the business- or errand-dress. It should, however, display no two incongruous colors, and had best be in one tint, except where a contrasting or harmonizing color is introduced in the way of ornament, in a bow at the neck or a flower upon the hat.

The dress for the promenade should be in perfect harmony with itself. One article should not be new and another shabby. The gloves may not be of one color, the bonnet of another, and the parasol of a third. All the colors worn should at least harmonize if they are not strictly identical.

The collars and cuffs must be of lace, the gloves of kid, selected to harmonize or contrast with the leading color of the dress, and perfect in fit. No jewelry should be worn save cuff-buttons, bracelets and ear-rings of plain gold, a watch-chain and handsome brooch.

The material of a walking-suit may be as rich or as plain as the wearer's taste may dictate or means justify, but it must always be well made and never allowed to grow shabby. It is better to avoid bright colors and use them only in decoration. Black has come to be adopted very generally for street-dresses; but while it is becoming for most individuals, it gives to the promenade a somewhat sombre look.

In the country walking-dresses must be made for service rather than display, and what would be perfectly appropriate for the streets of a city would be entirely out of place on the muddy, unpaved walks or paths of a small town or among the unpretending population of a country neighborhood.

The promenade-dress, whether for city or country, is always made short enough to clear the ground.

CARRIAGE-DRESS

The dress for a drive though the streets of a city or along a fashionable drive or park can scarcely be too rich in material. Silks, velvets and laces are all appropriate, with rich jewelry and costly furs.

The carriage-dress may be long enough to trail if fashion so indicates, though many prefer to use the short walking-dress length.

For country driving a different style of dress is required to protect against the mud or dust. It seems hardly necessary to describe the dress suitable for country driving, for each lady is capable of selecting for herself, bearing in mind that the dress is worn for protection and not for mere show.

If the lady drives herself, she will require wash-leather or cloth gloves, for handling the reins will ruin kid or thread ones.

RIDING-DRESS

There is no place where a handsome woman appears to better advantage than upon horseback. We will take it for granted that our lady has acquired properly the art of riding. Next she must be provided with a becoming habit. Her habit must fit perfectly without being tight. The skirt must be full and long enough to well cover the feet, while it is best to omit the extreme length, which subjects the dress to mud-splatterings and may prove a serious entanglement to the feet in case of accident.

A lady in donning the riding costume must take off all skirts and put on drawers of the same material as her habit. The boots must be stout and the gloves gauntleted.

Waterproof is the most serviceable cloth for a riding costume, though broadcloth is more dressy. Something lighter may be worn in summer. In the lighter costume a row or two of shot must be stitched in the bottom of the breadths of the left side to keep the skirt from blowing up in the wind.

The riding-dress is usually made to fit the waist closely and button nearly to the throat. Above a small collar or reverse (sic) on the waist is shown a plain linen collar, fastened at the throat with bright or black necktie. Coat sleeves should come to the wrist, with linen cuffs beneath them. No lace or embroidery is allowable in a riding costume.

It is well to have the waist attached to a skirt of the usual length and the long skirt fastened over it, so that if any mishap obliges the lady to dismount she may easily remove the long overskirt and still be properly dressed. [For a pattern, see LADIES' RIDING HABITS and LADIES' RIDING TROWSERS in Louis Devere's *THE HANDBOOK OF PRACTICAL CUTTING on the Centre Point System*. Although this was originally published about ten years earlier than the period under discussion, the basic riding habit did not change very rapidly in cut. *Ed.*]

The hair must be put up compactly, and neither curls nor veil should be allowed to stream in the wind. No jewelry save that absolutely required to fasten the dress, and that of the plainest kind, is allowable.

All ruffing, puffing or bows in the trimming of a riding-dress is out of place. Trimming, if used at all, must be put on in perfectly flat bands or be of braiding.

The shape of the hat will vary with the fashion, but it should always be plainly trimmed; and if feathers are worn, they must be fastened so that the wind cannot by any possibility blow them over their wearer's eyes.

VISITING AND RECEIVING CALLS

Calls may be made in either walking- or carriage-dress, always provided the carriage-dress is justified by the presence of the carriage itself. The dress should be of silk, with velvet cloak in winter and lace one in summer; collar and cuffs of the finest lace, light gloves, a full-dress bonnet and jewelry of gold, either dead, burnished or enameled, or of cameo or coral. Glittering stones are not worn by daylight.

A dress of black or neutral tint in which light colors are introduced only in small quantities is the most appropriate for a morning call, and the only one sure to be in harmony with the furniture and surroundings of the different reception-rooms against which it must be displayed.

DRESS FOR RECEIVING CALLS

The dress of a hostess differs with the occasion on which she is called to receive her guests, and also with the social position and means of the wearer.

A lady whose mornings are devoted to superintendence of domestic affairs may and should receive a casual caller in her ordinary morning-dress, which must be neat yet plain, devoid of superfluous ornaments or jewelry.

If a lady sets aside a special day for the reception of calls, she must be dressed with more care to do honor to her visitors. Her dress may be of silk or other goods suitable to the season or to her position, but must be of quiet colors and plainly worn.

White plain linen collar and cuffs belong to the plain morning-dress; lace should be worn with the ceremonious dress, and a certain amount of jewelry is admissible.

For New Year's or other calls of special significance the dress should be rich, and may be elaborately trimmed. If the parlors are closed and the gas lighted, full evening-dress is required.

DINNER-DRESS

We do not in this country, as in England, expose the neck and arms at a dinner-party. These should be covered, if not by the dress itself, then by lace or muslin overwaist or cape and sleeves.

[Nearly all the books agree about this, and even those which state that dinner or evening dresses may be cut lower also state that they must not be cut as low as those worn in England! – *Ed.*]

DRESS OF HOSTESS

The hostess' dress should be rich in material, but subdued in tone, in order that she may not eclipse any of her guests. A young hostess should wear a dress of rich silk, black or dark in color, with collar and cuffs of fine lace, and plain jewelry by daylight, or, if the dinner is by gaslight, glittering stones.

An elderly lady may wear satin, moire antique or velvet, with rich lace. If gloves are worn before dinner, they are withdrawn at the dinner-table.

DRESS OF GUESTS AT DINNER-PARTY

The dress of a guest at a dinner-party is less showy than that for evening; still, it may be very rich. Silks and velvets for winter and light, rich goods for summer, which latter may be worn over silk, are the most appropriate.

Young unmarried ladies should wear dresses of lighter materials and tints than married ones. Middle-aged and married ladies should wear silks heavier in quality and richer in tone, and elderly ladies satins, velvets and moire antiques.

All the light neutral tints and black, dark blue, purple, dark green, garnet, brown and fawn are suited for dinner wear. But whatever color the dress may be, it is best to try its effect by daylight and gaslight both, since many a color which will look well in daylight may look extremely ugly in artificial light.

[It is well to note that "the dinner-hour in cities where gentlemen are detained at their places of business during the day is ordinarily postponed until five, six or even seven, o'clock; but in the country and small towns it occurs at a much earlier hour". Also, "Guests may arrive at a ball at any time between the hours of nine and twelve. They should avoid going too early." – Ed.]

ORDINARY EVENING-DRESS

A lady should always be prepared for casual visitors in the evening. The house-dress should be tasteful and becoming, made with a certain amount of ornament and worn with lace and jewelry. Silks are the most appropriate for this dress, but all the heavy woolen dress fabrics for winter and the lighter lawns and organdies for summer, elegantly made, are suitable.

For winter the colors should be rich and warm, and knots of bright ribbon should be worn at the throat and in the hair. The latter should be dressed plainly, with no ornament save a ribbon. Artificial flowers are out of place, and glittering gems are only worn on more important occasions.

DRESS FOR EVENING CALL

Those who pay a casual evening call will dress in similar style, though somewhat more elaborately. More pains may be taken with the coiffure. A hood should not be worn unless it is intended to remove it during the call. Otherwise a full-dress bonnet must be upon the head.

DRESS FOR A SOCIAL PARTY

For the social evening-party the rules just given regarding dress will apply, save that somewhat more latitude is allowed in the choice of colors, materials, trimming, etc. Dresses should be worn covering the arms and shoulders; or if they are cut low in the neck and with short sleeves, puffed illusion waists or some similar device should be employed to cover the neck and arms.

Dark silks are very dressy – relieved by white lace and glittering gems are admirable. Gloves may or may not be worn. If worn, they should be white or of some light tint harmonizing with the dress.

THE SOIREE AND BALL

These two occasions call for the richest dress. The former usually requires dark, rich color and heavy material, the latter far lighter tints and goods. The richest velvets, the brightest and most delicate tints in silk, the most expensive laces, low neck and short sleeves, elaborate coiffures, the greatest display of gems, artificial flowers for the headdress, 'bouquet de corsage' and ornaments upon the skirt, natural ones in the hand bouquet – all belong more or less to these occasions.

Still, it is possible to be over-dressed. It is best to aim at being as well dressed as the rest, yet not to outdo others or render one's self conspicuous. A lady must also consider her years, her means, the importance of the occasion, her complexion, size and general costume in selecting for herself a dress for ball-room or soiree.

The colors of an evening-dress should always be tried by gaslight, for some tints which are beautiful by daylight lose all their character when worn in the evening, and look faded and hideous.

White kid gloves and white satin boots always belong to these costumes unless the overdress is of black lace, when black satin boots or slippers are required.

DRESS FOR CHURCH

The dress for church should be characterized by plainness and simplicity. It should be of dark, quiet colors for winter, and there should be no superfluous trimming or jewelry. It should, in fact, be the plainest of promenade-dresses, since church is not intended as a place for the display of elaborate toilets, and as no woman of consideration and right feeling would wish to make her own expensive and showy toilet an excuse to another woman, who could not afford to dress in a similar manner, for not attending divine worship.

DRESS FOR THE THEATRE

The ordinary promenade-dress is the suitable one for the theatre, with the addition of a handsome shawl or cloak, which may be thrown aside if it become uncomfortable. Either the bonnet or hat may be worn. In some cities it is customary to remove the bonnet in the theatre – a custom which is sanctioned by good sense and a kind of consideration of those who sit behind, but which has not yet the authority of etiquette. The dress should be, in all respects, quiet and plain, without any attempt at display. Gloves should be dark, harmonizing with the costume.

DRESS FOR LECTURE AND CONCERT

Lecture- and concert-halls call for a little more elaboration in toilet. Silk is the most appropriate material for the dress, and should be worn with lace collar and cuffs and jewelry. If the bonnet is worn, it should be handsome; and if it is removed, the coiffure should be somewhat elaborately made, with either ribbons or flowers. White or light kid gloves should be upon the hands. A rich shawl or velvet promenade cloak or opera cloak is an appropriate finish. The latter may be kept on the shoulders during the evening. The handkerchief should be fine and delicate; the fan of a color to harmonize with the dress.

DRESS FOR THE OPERA

The opera calls out the richest of all costumes. The lady goes to the opera not only to see but to be seen, and her dress must be adopted with a full realization of the thousand gaslights which will bring out its merits and defects, and of the hundred lorgnettes which will be no less spying.

The material of the dress should be heavy enough to bear the crush of the place, rich in color and splendid in its arrangement and trimming. The headdress should be of flowers, ribbons, lace or feathers – whatever may be the prevailing style – and the head must be uncovered. If, however, it is found necessary to have the head protected, a bonnet of the lightest, daintiest character must be adopted. If a bonnet is worn, the arms and neck must be covered.

Jewelry of the heaviest and richest description is admissible in this place, and there is no occasion when the glitter of gems will be seen to better advantage.

White kids or those of light, delicate tints are indispensable.

A most important adjunct to an opera-costume is the cloak or wrap. This may be white or of some brilliant color. White and gold, scarlet and gold, green and gold or Roman stripe are all very effective when worn with appropriate dresses. White ermine capes are beautiful when lined with white satin or colored silk and finished with heavy white cord and tassels.

Lace, either black or white, may be adopted with great advantage in an opera-dress. Pink, purple, orange and most light tints require black lace, while the neutral shades may be worn with either white or black.

Blue and yellow should both be avoided in an opera-dress, as neither bears the light well. Green requires gold as a contrasting color; crimson, black.

The lorgnette, the fan, the bouquet and dainty handkerchief must all have due consideration and be in keeping with the other portions of the dress. Thus a lady in pink should avoid a bouquet in which scarlet flowers predominate.

CROQUET AND SKATING COSTUMES

Skating is to winter what croquet is to summer, and the requirements of their costumes, in all but material, are similar. Both call for a greater brilliancy in coloring than any other out-of-door costume. They should both be short, displaying a handsomely fitting but stout boot. Both should be arranged, by the use of close-fitting sacques, to leave the arms perfectly free.

Croquet gloves should be soft and washable; skating gloves thick and warm. Kid is not suitable on either occasion.

The hat for croquet should have a broad brim, so as to shield the face from the sun and render a parasol unnecessary.

Velvet trimmed with fur, with turban hat of the same, and gloves and boots also fur bordered, combine to make the most elegant skating costume imaginable. But any of the soft, warm bright-colored woolen fabrics are quite as suitable, if not so rich. A costume of Scotch plaid is in excellent taste. If cold tints, such as blue or green, are worn, they should be relieved with trimmings of warm, dark furs. Silk is not suitable for a skating costume.

White furs should only be worn by experienced skaters, for they easily become soiled by the novitiate in tumbles upon the ice.

The boot should be amply loose or the wearer will suffer with cold or frozen feet.

COSTUMES FOR COUNTRY AND SEA-SIDE

Let the show wardrobe be ever so numerous, there must be a certain number of costumes suited for ordinary wear and to do more or less battle with the elements. Thus, dresses, while they may be somewhat brighter in tint than good taste would justify in the streets of a city, must yet be durable in quality and of wash material. The brim of the hat should be broad enough to protect the wearer from the sun. The fashion of making hats of shirred muslin is a very sensible one, as it enables them to be done up when they are soiled. The boots must be stout and serviceable. A waterproof is an indispensible article to the sojourner at country resorts.

YACHTING COSTUMES

Young ladies wear either flannel suits of navy blue, or white, plainly but prettily trimmed with woollen braid, jaunty sailor hats, 'gants de Suede', and thick boots. A large parasol is necessary for comfort. A black silk suit is the next desirable costume to one of flannel. Warm shawls should be provided, no matter how oppressive the day. The wind is as changeable as the fair women who trust to it, and a yacht may put out to sea in a calm to return in a gale.

BATHING COSTUMES

A bathing-dress is best made of flannel [wool – *Ed.*]. A soft gray tint is the prettiest, as it does not so soon fade and grow ugly from contact with the salt water. It may be trimmed with bright worsted braid. The best form is the loose sacque or the yoke waist, both of them to be belted in and falling about midway between the knee and the ankle. Full trowsers gathered in a band at the ankle, an oilskin cap to protect the hair, which becomes harsh in the salt water, and merino socks of the color of the dress complete the costume.

Any other material than flannel becomes limp and unsightly after being worn for a short time.

TRAVELLING-DRESS

The first consideration in a travelling-dress is comfort; the second, protection from the dust and stains of travel.

In summer, for a short journey, a large linen duster or overdress may be put on over the ordinary dress, and in winter a waterproof cloak may be used in the same way.

But a lady making an extensive journey will find it convenient to have a travelling-suit prepared expressly. Linen is still useful in summer, as the dust is so easily shaken from it and it can be readily washed. In winter a waterproof dress and sacque are the most serviceable.

There are a variety of materials especially adapted for travelling costumes, of soft neutral tints and smooth surfaces, which do not catch dust, these should be made up plainly and always quite short.

The underskirts should always be colored woolen in winter, linen in summer. Nothing displays vulgarity and want of breeding so completely as the white petticoat in traveling.

Gloves should be of Lisle thread in summer and cloth in winter, never of kid. Boots thick soled, stout and durable. The hat or bonnet must be plainly trimmed and completely protected by a large veil. Velvet is unfit for a traveling-hat, as it catches and retains the dust.

Plain linen collar and cuffs finish the costume. The hair should be put up in the plainest manner possible. Curls or fancy braids are inadmissible.

A waterproof and a warm woolen shawl are indispensible in travelling. Also a satchel or hand-basket, in which should be kept a change of collars, cuffs, gloves, handkerchiefs, towels [probably a reference to sanitary towels or napkins – *Ed.*] and toilet articles. A lunch-basket is sometimes desirable.

A traveling-dress should be well supplied with pockets. The waterproof should have large pockets; so should the sacque. The pocket of the dress should be deep and large.

In an underskirt there should be provided a pocket in which to carry all money not needed for immediate use. The latter may be entrusted to the 'portemonnaie' in the ordinary pocket, or in the bosom of the dress.

THE WEDDING-DRESS

Her dress may be of silk heavily corded, moire antique, brocade, satin or plain silk, or lace, merino, alpaca, crape, lawn or muslin. Her veil may be of lace, tulle or illusion but it must be long and full. It may or may not descend over the face. The flowers of the bridal wreath and bouquet must be orange blossoms, either natural or artificial, or other white flowers.

The dress is high and the arms are covered. No jewelry is worn save diamonds or pearls. Slippers of white satin and gloves of kid complete the dress.

The style of great simplicity in bridal toilettes, adopted in continental Europe is more commendable than that of England and America, where the bridal dress is made as expensive and as heavy with rich and costly lace as it is possible to make it.

DRESS OF BRIDESMAIDS

The dresses of the bridesmaids are less elaborate than that of the bride. They should be also of white, but they may be trimmed with delicately-colored flowers and ribbons. White tulle worn over pale pink or blue silk, and caught up with blush-roses or forget-me-nots, with 'bouquet de corsage' and hand-bouquet of the same, makes a charming bridesmaid's costume.

The bridesmaids may or may not wear veils, but in case they wear them they should be shorter than that of the bride.

TRAVELING-DRESS OF BRIDE

The traveling-dress of a bride should be of silk, or of any of the fine fabrics for walking-dresses. It should be of some neutral tint, and bonnet and gloves should match in color. A bridal traveling costume may be somewhat more elaborately trimmed than an ordinary traveling-dress; though, if the bride wishes to attract as little attention as possible, she will not make herself conspicuous by too showy a garb.

A bride is frequently married in traveling costume; but when this is the case, the wedding is a private one, and the bridal pair set out at once upon their journey.

SECOND MARRIAGE OF A WIDOW

A widow is never married in white. Widows and brides of middle age choose delicate neutral tints, with white gloves and white lace collar and cuffs. The costumes of the bridesmaids must take their tone from that of the bride, and be neither lighter, richer nor gayer than hers.

Bride and bridesmaids wear their wedding-dresses at the wedding reception.

DRESS OF GUESTS AT WEDDING-RECEPTION

The guests at an evening reception should wear full evening-dress. No one should attend in black or wear any sign of mourning. Those in mourning lay aside black for lavender or gray.

For a morning reception the dress should be the richest street costume, with white gloves. If at the morning reception the blinds are closed and the gas lighted, then evening-dress is worn by the guests.

THE TROUSSEAU

The trousseau may be as large and expensive as the circumstances of the bride will justify, but this expense is mainly put upon outside garments. There are certain requisite articles which must be supplied in a requisite number, and these all brides must have, and of a certain similarity in general character and make. They may be set down as follows:

Twelve chemises, six elaborately trimmed and six more plainly made.

Twelve pairs of drawers, made in sets with the chemises, and matching them in trimming.

Six fine and six plain night-dresses.

Six corset-covers, three finely finished.

Four pairs of corsets, one pair white embroidered, two plain white and one pair colored, the latter to be used in travelling.

One dozen pair of fine thread hose, one dozen of heavy cotton and one dozen of fine merino hose are none too many.

Six trimmed skirts and six plain ones.

Two balmoral skirts, one handsome and the other plain.

Six flannel skirts, three of them handsomely embroidered.

Four white dressing-sacques, two of them of flannel.

Two loose wrappers of chintz or cashmere.

Six sets of linen collars and cuffs for morning wear.

Six sets of lace or embroidered collars and cuffs.

One dozen plain handkerchiefs, one dozen fine handkerchiefs and six embroidered or lace trimmed.

Walking-boots, gaiters and slippers of various styles.

Two pairs of white kid gloves, two of light and two of dark tints, with others of thread and cloth.

Of dresses there are required — morning-dresses, walking-suits, carriage-dresses, one traveling-dress, one waterproof suit, one very handsome suit to return bridal calls, and last but not least the bridal-dress, which has already been referred to. These dresses may be multiplied in number according to the means and needs of the bride.

[Not to mention cloaks, shawls, capes, bonnets, hats, etc. – *Ed*]

[Many etiquette books state that the people of the United States have settled upon no prescribed periods for the wearing of mourning garments, but instead wear them to a greater or lesser degree depending upon their grief. *Ed*]

DEEP MOURNING

Deep mourning requires the heaviest black of serge, bombazine, lustreless alpaca, de laine, merino or similar heavy clinging material, with collar and cuffs of crape. A widow wears a bonnet-cap of white tarletan, known as the "widow's cap."

Mourning garments are made in the severest simplicity. They should have little or no trimming; no flounces, ruffles or bows are allowable. If the dress is not made *en suite*, then a long or square shawl of barege or cashmere with crape border is worn.

The bonnet is of black crape; a hat is inadmissible. The veil is of crape or berege (*sic*) with heavy border. Black gloves and black-bordered handkerchief.

In winter dark furs may be worn with the deepest mourning. Jewelry is strictly forbidden, and all pins, buckles, etc., must be of jet.

SECOND MOURNING
(That worn after the initial period. – *Ed*)

Lustreless alpaca may be worn in second mourning, with white collar and cuffs. The crape veil is laid aside for net or tulle, but the jet jewelry is still retained.

LESSER DEGREES OF MOURNING

A still less degree of mourning is indicated by black and white, purple and gray, or a combination of these colors. Crape is still retained in bonnet trimming, and crape flowers may be added.

Light gray, white and black, and light shades of lilac indicate a slight mourning. Black lace bonnet with white or violet flowers supercedes crape, and jet and gold jewelry is worn.

It is poor economy to buy cheap and flimsy materials for mourning. Only the best black goods wear well without becoming rusty and shabby. Foulards make serviceable half-mourning dresses, either as wrappers or walking-suits.

Ladies invited to funeral ceremonies should always wear a black dress, even if they are not in mourning; and it is bad taste to appear with a gay bonnet or shawl, as if for a festive occasion.

The mourning for children under twelve years of age is white in summer and gray in winter, with black trimmings, belt, sleeve-ruffles and bonnet-ribbons.

GLOSSARY

Alpaca – long, fine hair from South American goats mixed with silk or cotton; silk gives a lustre fabric, and cotton a lustreless.

Aesthetic dress – a loose, limp style adopted by some Englishwomen as a protest against corsets and tight bodices.

Balayeuse – a "street sweeper" or dust ruffle basted inside the hem of the skirt, removable and washable.

Balmoral skirt – actually a petticoat meant to be seen when the outer skirt is looped up.

Basque – any bodice that extends below the waistline.

Blonde lace – fine French bobbin lace with a floral pattern on a net ground.

Body-waist – see "waist".

Bombazine – dress material made of silk and wool with a twilled surface, also out of cotton and worsted with a dull surface.

Bones – stays made of whalebone.

Bonnet – headcovering fitting over the back and top of the head and tied with strings under the chin.

Bonnet-cap – probably a "Capote", popular in the U. S. from 1830-90's; had a stiff brim framing the face, a soft gathered crown, and ribbon bows tied at the side or under the chin.

Breakfast-cap – morning-cap, dainty cap of lace, tulle and ribbon worn on the back of the head, indoors.

Broadcloth – a cloth made of fine merino yarn in plain twill weave, heavily milled, with a dress face finish.

Bust pads – cotton pads used to fill out the shoulder hollow and give a smooth, full front to the bodice.

Cambric – a very fine white linen, originally made at Cambray in Flanders.

Cashmere – extremely fine soft wool made from Indian Kashmir goat hair.

Chemise – undermost garment for the top part of the body, usually of linen.

Chintz – cotton cloth printed in various colors, with a glazed surface.

Circular – long cape or mantle, often of silk or satin and lined with fur.

Combinations – underwear combining the chemise and drawers; Jaeger introduced these for women in 1877.

Corded silk – silk with a lengthwise cord made by weaving a thick silk over a coarse thread.

Corsage – the upper part or bodice of a dress.

Corset – (or stays) undergarment with whalebone or steel ribs compressing the natural waist.

Corset-cover – (or camisole) underbodice worn over stays to protect the dress.

Crape – black silk fabric, or transparent crimped silk gauze, used for mourning clothes.

Cuff-buttons – small buttons often of mother-of-pearl, sewn on cuff, used to fasten the cuff.

Cuirass bodice – a basque with long points front and back and curving up over the hips on the sides.

Dead gold – unburnished, or gold without lustre.

De laine – crepe de laine, slightly crinkled sheer wool fabric made with crepe-twisted yarn.

Dolman – a mantle, cape-like (or longer, like a cloak) in back but with a dolman sleeve in front.

Dolman sleeve – cut in one piece with the sidepiece of the garment and hanging loose.

Drawers – underpants, usually trimmed with lace.

Dress holder – device made with two pendant chains ending in clips, used for holding up the skirt and/or train when crossing the street.

Dress-waist – see "waist".

Dressing-sacque – loose-fitting hip-length jacket worn in the boudoir.

Duchesse dress – referred to as an alternative name for a princess style dress, but this is not its usual meaning.

Duster – long summer overcoat or overdress made of silk or alpaca, sometimes caped and belted.

En suite – made of matching fabric.

Flannel – woollen fabric with a loose weave.

Foulard – soft, light-weight silk in twill with small design.

Gaiters – covering for the ankle and small of the leg spreading out over the upper part of the shoe or boot and buttoned on the outer side.

Gants de Suede – suede gloves.

Garniture – trimmings: ruffles, lace, ribbons, bows.

Gauging – shirring, a series of close parallel running stitches so that the material in between is fixed as gathers, used as trim.

Gauntlet – an above the wrist glove with a wide flaring cuff; thus, "gauntleted".

Gore – a construction method used in skirts where panels are cut narrow at the top and wide at the bottom to provide shaping without darts.

Illusion – fine tulle or net used for veils, etc.

Jet – lignite, a black mineral which polishes to a high lustre.

Kid – skin of a young goat.

Lawn – a fine white linen similar to cambric.

Linen – strong, lustrous fabric made of flax fibers.

Lisle thread – a fine, hard twisted, long staple cotton thread, 2 or more ply.

Lorgnettes – a pair of eye- or opera-glasses on a handle, usually decorated.

Lustreless gold – see "Dead gold".

Marseilles – reversible fabric in Jacquard weave with raised woven pattern, all white or white with colored design.

Merino – wool made from merino sheep, very fine and resembling cashmere.

Moire antique – a waved or watered effect used especially on a corded silk.

Morning-dress – housedress.

Muslin – general term for light, delicately woven cotton fabric with a downy nap.

Night-dress – a loose nightgown of cotton, linen or silk worn in bed only.

Oilskin cap – cap of cotton fabric coated on one side with vegetable oils and pigments mixed with a clay filler, usually bright yellow.

Opera cloak or wrap – usually full length and made of elaborate fabric trimmed with fur or feathers.

Organdy – soft, sheer muslin with a permanently crisp finish.

Over-sack – or sack overcoat; a long, loose overcoat; also, a raincoat.

Paints – cosmetics or make-up, as in 'painted woman'.

Panier/pannier/pannier drape – piece of fabric added to bodice or waistline and draped over the hips and pulled to the back.

Parasol – ornamental umbrella used to ward off the sun, not waterproofed.

Petticoat-suspender corset – a corset with buttons about an inch from the bottom from which a petticoat could be suspended.

Pique – cotton with raised cord or welts, known as wales, crossing in the fabric.

Plumet petticoat – narrow petticoat with ruffles at the back taking the place of a bustle.

Polonaise – an overdress with fitted bodice whose sides and/or back could be pulled up like draperies.

Portemonnaie – "French" purse, a fold-over wallet with a change purse in one end.

Princess style dress – basic cut characterized by continuous vertical panels from hem to neckline, shaped to the body through the torso and having no waist seam.

Promenade cloak – used when out walking and simpler than a carriage cloak.

Puffed illusion waist – a very sheer blouse; see "illusion".

Reverse – misprint; should be 'revers', a collar or turned-back edge.

Rouleau – tube stitched at regular intervals to make puffs, used as a trim.

Roman stripe – horizontal stripes, varied in size and grouped together with no contrast background.

Rusty – cheap black fabric turned reddish because of the unstable dyes used.

Sack/sacque/sac – a loose garment often with a sac-back consisting of two deep box pleats (Watteau style); could be a dressing-gown, or in different materials a loose overcoat (see "over-sack", "wrapper").

Sacque jacket – short, loose jacket with full sleeves, worn at home, trimmed with lace (see "dressing-sacque"), or on the street trimmed with fur (also a fitted sack jacket, a street jacket but not loose).

Satchel – (in this case) a small basket used as a handbag, lined with fabric and often with leather handles.

Serge – twill-weave fabric made of wool with prominent diagonal ribs on both sides of the cloth.

Shirred muslin – having three or more rows of gathers to produce fullness.

Shooting jacket – informal morning coat (worn by men).

Shot – buckshot sewn in to weight the material.

Stays – corset; term also used for the bones sewn into the seams of the foundation garment to hold the shape.

Steels – half-circle hoops fitted into horizontal channels to hold out the back part of the skirt.

Surtout – an overcoat or greatcoat.

Talma – elaborate mantle or cloak, with or without sleeves, for evening wear; named after a famous French actor of the Consulate and Empire periods.

Tapes – tapes or tabs sewn into the seam of the skirt and used to pull the fullness to the back.

Tarletan – thin, heavily sized cotton muslin.

Tulle – very fine silk net used for veils and trimmings.

Tunic – a loose-fitting overdress or overskirt; also an over-blouse.

Tunic dress – a dress with a tight fitting bodice and a loose overskirt which was pulled up to expose the underskirt.

Turban hat – an adaptation of an Indian man's turban.

Ulster – a loose, ankle-length coat with a cape.

Vandyke – a border of lace or saw-tooth edged fabric.

Waist – term used for: a bodice, a blouse, a shirt-waist, a body-waist, or a dress-waist, the upper part of a dress above the skirt; also an under-blouse to which skirts were attached by means of buttons; and even to indicate the waist-line (depending upon the situation).

Walking jacket – a three-quarter length jacket, often fur trimmed and decorated with braid, worn especially by younger women.

Wash-leather – a soft leather, usually of split sheepskin, dressed to imitate chamois.

Waterproof – term used for a large garment (raincoat or cape) which was waterproof; rubberized treatment of material; treatment of material with chemicals to render it waterproof (see waterproofing recipe below).

Watteau fold – a sack back with deep box pleats forming a loose back.

Widow's cap – headdress arched on either side of the forehead to form a 'widow's peak', often draped with a black veil upon going outdoors.

Worsted (braid) – smooth, tightly twisted wool yarn (used to make braided cord trimmings).

Wrapper – term used for a loose fitting overcoat, also for a woman's dressing-gown.

Yoke Waist – yoke blouse, made with a yoke front and back.

WATERPROOFING

The following is from Devere's *The Handbook of Practical Cutting*. It is included to give a better idea of what was meant by waterproof fabric.

RECEIPT FOR WATERPROOFING

We here give a receipt for making every kind of woollen, cotton, or linen material waterproof, and it will be found, if practised, of immense value and advantage to the trade.

Take one ounce of alum, and dissolve it in a quart of water: in another vessel dissolve one ounce of acetate or sugar of lead, also in a quart of water; when the alum and lead are entirely dissolved, empty one vessel into that which contains the other; mix them well together by stirring them with a stick, then leave it for a time to settle, and when a deposit is formed at the bottom, pour the liquid gently off into another vessel, leaving the waste deposit behind. The liquid part being now ready, immerse the material to be rendered waterproof, leaving it a little time to soak, then press it with the hands to get some of the water out, and hang it on a line to dry.

This manner of rendering materials waterproof, does not alter either the colour or the pliability of the material: it also allows the escape of the perspiration.

There will be a faint smell at first, something like vinegar, but it will go off in about two days.

To prove the efficacy of the recipe, try first on a small piece of cloth or alpaca; you will find that you may carry water about in it, without a single drop passing through.

The quantities given above will be sufficient to waterproof a Paletot or coat. We must remind our readers that very coarse stout clothes are not suited for this operation, which is most successful when applied to finer materials, such as Tweeds, etc., etc., which it will render sufficiently waterproof to protect the wearer against the effects of an ordinary shower, though indeed, unless the cloth was very fine, and the waterproofing very well done, it might not be proof against a whole day's heavy rain.

BIBLIOGRAPHY

Batterberry, Michael & Ariane. *Fashion: Mirror of History.* 1982. N.Y.

Bettmann, Otto. *The Good Old Days – They Were Terrible.* 1974. N.Y.

Bigelow, Marybelle. *Fashions in History: Apparel in the Western World.* 1970. Minnesota.

Bradley, Carolyn. *Western World Costume.* 1954. New York.

Buck, Anne. *Victorian Costume.* 1984. U.K.

E. Butterick & Co's Catalogue: Summer 1879. New York.

The Butterick Co. *The Dressmaker,* 1911 and 1916 rev. New York.

Butterick, E. *The Delineator: August 1881.* New York.

Calasibetta, Charlotte. *Fairchild's Dictionary of Fashion.* 1975. New York.

Carens, Edith. *Dressmaking Self Taught.* 1911. Jacksonville.

Catalogue of Domestic Fashions: Fall 1880. New York.

Caufield, S. F. & Blanche Saward. *Encyclopedia of Victorian Needlework.* 1882/1886. 1985. 2 vols. New York.

Church, Ella. *The Home Needle.* 1882. New York.

Collard, Eileen. *Cut & Construction of Women's 19th Century Dress – Pt. 4: Rise & Fall of the Bustle.* 1979. Canada.

Collard, Eileen. *Robertson & Bros: Guide to Dressmaking & Fancy Work (ca. 1876).* 1977. Canada.

Contini, Mila. *Fashions from Ancient Egypt to the Present Day.* 1965. N.Y.

Costume for Sport. 1963. Manchester, U. K.

Cunnington, C. W. & P. E., and Charles Beard. *A Dictionary of English Costume 900-1900.* 1976. London.

Decorum: A Practical Treatise on Etiquette & Dress of the Best American Society. 1878. Chicago.

Devere, Louis. *The Handbook of Practical Cutting on the Centre Point System (1866).* 1986. Lopez Island.

Duffey, Mrs. E. B. *Ladies' & Gentlemen's Etiquette.* 1877. Philadelphia.

Frost, S. Annie. *Ladies' Guide to Needle Work (1877).* 1986. Lopez Island.

Furnas, J. C. *The Americans: A Social History of the United States 1587-1914.* 1969. N.Y.

Harper's Bazar: January 1877.

Harper's Bazar: September 1878.

Kidwell, Claudia. *Cutting a Fashionable Fit.* 1979. Washington, D. C.

The Lady's Maid; Her Duties & How to Perform Them. Houlston's Industrial Library. 1877. London.

Lester, Kathleen. *Historic Costume.* 1942. Peoria.

Lord & Taylor: Clothing & Furnishings, 1881. 1971. Princeton.

Markun, Leo. *Mrs. Grundy* (1930). 1968. N. Y.

Morison, Samuel. *The Oxford History of the American People.* 1965. N. Y.

O'Day, Deirdre. *Victorian Jewellery.* 1962 rev. London.

Peterson's Magazine: 1879.

Picken, Mary B. *The Language of Fashion.* 1939. N. Y.

Polokoff, et al. *Generations of Americans: A History of the United States.* 1976. N.Y.

Rayne, Mrs. M. L. *Gems of Deportment.* 1881. Chicago.

Robinson, Nugent. *Collier's Cyclopedia of Commercial & Social Information.* 1882. N. Y.

Ross, Ishbel. *Crusades & Crinolines.* 1963. N. Y.

Tarrant, Naomi. *Great Grandmother's Clothes: Women's Fashions in the 1880's.* 1986. Edinburgh.

Urdang, Laurence (ed.). *The Timetables of American History.* 1981. N. Y.

Ward, Mrs. H. O. *Sensible Etiquette of the Best Society.* 1878. Philadelphia.

Wilcox, R. Turner. *The Mode in Costume.* 1948. N. Y.

Young, John. *Our Deportment or Manners, Conduct & Dress of the Most Refined Society.* 1879. Detroit.